SOUVENIR PROGRAMS OF FIVE GREAT WORLD SERIES

1914, 1917, 1919, 1926, 1934

Edited by

Bert Randolph Sugar

Dover Publications, In
New York

Published in Canada by General Publishing Company, Ltd., 30 Lesmill Road, Don Mills, Toronto, Ontario.

Published in the United Kingdom by Constable and Company, Ltd., 10 Orange Street, London WC2H 7EG.

Souvenir Programs of Five Great World Series, first published by Dover Publications, Inc., in 1980, is a new selection of original programs. The editor wrote the preface and the commentaries that precede the programs specially for the present volume. The covers of the programs, originally in color, are here reproduced in black and white.

The composite box scores on pages 2, 26, 64, 124 and 152 are reprinted here by permission of Sports Products, Inc., from *The World Series* by Richard M. Cohen, David S. Neft, Roland T. Johnson and Jordan A. Deutsch (New York, 1976).

International Standard Book Number: 0-486-23858-X
Library of Congress Catalog Card Number: 79-57224

Manufactured in the United States of America
Dover Publications, Inc.
180 Varick Street
New York, N.Y. 10014

PREFACE

The World Series is at once the most prestigious and the most pretentious event on the American landscape. The most prestigious because no other event has captured the headlines or the imagination of America for so long a period of time or so intensely. The most pretentious because it holds itself out to be a competition for the baseball championship of the world, when it is, in reality, only for the championship of the northeastern quadrant of the Western Hemisphere. (However, baseball men, with more than a small measure of conceit, still proudly defend it as the international championship. George Steinbrenner, Yankee owner, provided the official party line when challenged on its parochialism: "Well, we beat everybody who showed up.")

But the ideas that the World Series is played for the championship of the world and that it has always been between the winners of the National and American Leagues are just two of several misconceptions surrounding what has been called everything from "The Whirled Series" by Walt Kelly to "The World Serious" by Ring Lardner; and called The Autumn Classic" or World Series by millions of fans who find it the fitting climax to each baseball season.

For, according to Al Spink of *The Sporting New*, "The World's Series in baseball was first played in 1884, back when baseball was still two words and Pittsburgh didn't have an 'H' to hiss in." Moreover, Spink was to write 37 years after the inception of the so-called world's series (small "w", small "s"), "From 1884 until 1890, when the Brotherhood war broke up the contests, the series was fought out annually between the champion of the National League and the American Association." By 1892, "the winners of a divided season in the National League met for the title [and] from 1894 until 1897 the Temple Cup games between the first and second teams in the National League were played for the trophy," Spink concluded. So much for the myth concerning the start of the event known as the World Series.

The world will little note nor long remember those 12 Series. All that remains of them are a few write-ups in yellowing old papers and fewer memories of children grown old.

But in 1903 the World Series, as we have come to know it, began to take form and flight. For that was the year in which Barney Dreyfuss, owner of the Pittsburg Pirates, winners of three successive National League pennants, issued a challenge to Harry Killilea, president of the Boston Pilgrims, to play a best-five-out-of-nine series for the "world's championship." The Pilgrims surprised the Pirates, and the National League, by winning five out of eight—and the so-called championship of the world.

The next year the Pilgrims repeated in the American League and issued a challenge to the new National League champions, the New York Giants. But the president of the Giants, John T. Brush, refused to permit his Giants to play, branding the American League a "minor league" and issuing a statement that "by winning the National League pennant the Giants had already won the championship."

But Brush, prodded by strong public opinion, soon saw the error of his ways. Working within the framework of the National Agreement he had helped to draft, major league baseball established a best-of-seven series. Ironically, Brush's Giants were the *first* World Champions as we know them today, winners of a five-game Series against the Philadelphia Athletics in 1905.

Today, some 75 World Series later, the Series is still with us, the most enduring sports spectacle on the American—if not the world—scene. It has produced its memorable moments, its unlikely heroes and its great plays and players. But more importantly, it has grown with America, and no longer need be referred to in small letters; for the World Series is not only to be referred to in capitals, everything about it is caps.

This book of great World Series programs is not only a celebration of some of those moments, heroes and players that have made the Series what it is today—an event which stands alone among sporting events—but also a reaffirmation that baseball and the World Series are recurrent, and therefore imperishable.

We are indebted to Ike Kuhns for making programs of these five great World Series available to us, and to baseball which, with all its pretensions, has worn well with the passage of time.

BERT RANDOLPH SUGAR

Chappaqua, New York
October 17, 1979

CONTENTS

1914

Boston Braves
vs.
Philadelphia Athletics

1914 WORLD SERIES COMPOSITE BOX

	Wins	Composite Line Score												
Boston Braves (N.L.)	4	0	3	0	2	3	3	0	1	1	2	0	1	– 16
Philadelphia Athletics (A.L.)	0	1	1	0	1	1	0	0	0	0	2	0	0	– 6

	Regular Season			
Manager	W	L	Pct.	G. Ahead
George Stallings	94	59	.614	10½
Connie Mack	99	53	.651	8½

BATTING AND FIELDING

WORLD SERIES STATISTICS

BOSTON BRAVES	Pos	G	AB	R	H	2B	3B	HR	RBI	BB	SO	SB	BA	SA	PO	A	E
Butch Schmidt	1b	4	**17**	2	5	0	0	0	2	0	2	1	.294	.294	**52**	3	0
Johnny Evers	2b	4	16	2	**7**	0	0	0	2	2	2	1	.438	.438	8	16	**1**
Rabbit Maranville	ss	4	13	1	4	0	0	0	**3**	1	1	**2**	.308	.308	7	13	**1**
Charlie Deal	3b	4	16	1	2	2	0	0	0	0	0	**2**	.125	.250	6	11	0
Herbie Moran	rf	3	13	2	1	1	0	0	0	1	1	1	.077	.154	2	0	**1**
Possum Whitted	cf	4	14	2	3	0	**1**	0	2	3	1	1	.214	.357	5	0	0
Joe Connolly	lf	3	9	1	1	0	0	0	1	1	1	0	.111	.111	2	2	**1**
Hank Gowdy	c	4	11	**3**	6	**3**	**1**	**1**	**3**	**5**	1	1	**.545**	**1.273**	31	4	0
Les Mann	rf-pr-ph-lf	3	7	1	2	0	0	0	1	0	1	0	.286	.286	1	0	0
Ted Cather	lf	1	5	0	0	0	0	0	0	0	1	0	.000	.000	2	0	0
Josh Devore	ph	1	1	0	0	0	0	0	0	0	1	0	.000	.000			
Larry Gilbert	ph	1	0	0	0	0	0	0	0	1	0	0	—	—			
Red Smith		Did not play—broken ankle.															
Bert Whaling		Did not play															
Oscar Dugey		Did not play															
Billy Martin		Did not play															
Dick Rudolph	p	2	6	1	2	0	0	0	0	1	1	0	.333	.333	0	3	0
Bill James	p	2	4	0	0	0	0	0	0	0	4	0	.000	.000	0	5	0
Letty Tyler	p	1	3	0	0	0	0	0	0	0	1	0	.000	.000	1	5	0
Dick Crutcher		Did not play															
Otto Hess		Did not play															
Paul Strand		Did not play															
George Davis		Did not play															
Gene Cooreham		Did not play															
Dick Cottrell		Did not play															
team total		4	135	16	33	6	2	1	14	15	18	9	.244	.341	117	62	4

Double Plays—4
Left on Bases—27

REGULAR SEASON STATISTICS

BOSTON BRAVES		Main Pos	G	AB	R	H	2B	3B	HR	RBI	BB	SO	SB	BA	SA
Butch Schmidt		1b	147	537	67	153	17	9	1	71	43	55	14	.285	.356
Johnny Evers		2b	139	491	81	137	20	3	1	40	87	26	12	.279	.338
Rabbit Maranville		ss	156	586	74	144	23	6	4	78	45	56	28	.246	.326
Charlie Deal		3b	79	257	17	54	13	2	0	23	20	23	4	.210	.276
Herbie Moran	a	of	41	154	24	41	3	1	0	4	17	11	4	.266	.299
Possum Whitted	b	of-2b	66	218	36	57	11	4	2	31	18	18	10	.261	.376
Joe Connolly		of	120	399	64	122	28	10	9	65	49	36	12	.306	.494
Hank Gowdy		c	128	366	42	89	17	6	3	46	48	40	14	.243	.347
Les Mann		of	126	389	44	96	16	11	4	40	24	50	9	.247	.375
Ted Cather	c	of	50	145	19	43	4	0	1	27	7	28	7	.297	.400
Josh Devore	d	of	51	128	22	29	2	0	1	5	18	14	2	.227	.281
Larry Gilbert		of	72	224	32	60	6	1	5	25	26	34	3	.268	.371
Red Smith	e	3b	60	207	30	65	17	1	3	37	28	24	4	.314	.449
Bert Whaling		c	60	172	18	36	7	0	0	12	21	28	2	.209	.250
Oscar Dugey		of-2b	58	109	17	21	2	0	1	10	10	15	10	.193	.239
Billy Martin		ss	1	3	0	0	0	0	0	0	0	0	0	.000	.000
Dick Rudolph		p	43	120	10	15	4	1	0	8	11	19	1	.125	.175
Bill James		p	49	129	9	33	3	0	0	9	0	20	0	.256	.279
Letty Tyler		p	38	94	6	19	1	0	0	4	4	20	0	.202	.213
Dick Crutcher		p	33	54	5	8	1	0	0	3	4	15	1	.148	.167
Otto Hess		p-1b	31	47	5	11	1	0	1	6	1	11	0	.234	.319
Paul Strand		p	18	24	2	8	2	0	0	3	0	2	0	.333	.417
George Davis		p	9	18	1	3	0	0	0	2	2	6	0	.167	.167
Gene Cooreham		p	15	10	0	1	0	0	0	0	1	6	0	.100	.100
Dick Cottrell		p	1	0	0	0	0	0	0	0	0	0	0	—	—
team total			158	**5206**	657	1307	213	60	35	**572**	**502**	617	139	.251	.335

a—from Cincinnati
b—from St. Louis (N)
c—from St. Louis (N)
d—from Philadelphia (N)
e—from Brooklyn
Wilson Collins (of), Tommy Griffith (of), Clarence Kraft (lb), Jim Murray (of), Clancy Tyler (c), Tom Hughes (p), Dolf Luque (p), Hub Perdue (p) also played for the Braves during the season

WORLD SERIES STATISTICS

PHILADELPHIA ATHLETICS	Pos	G	AB	R	H	2B	3B	HR	RBI	BB	SO	SB	BA	SA	PO	A	E
Stuffy McInnis	1b	4	14	2	2	1	0	0	0	3	3	0	.143	.214	50	2	0
Eddie Collins	2b	4	14	0	3	0	0	0	1	2	1	1	.214	.214	9	12	**1**
Jack Barry	ss	4	14	1	1	0	0	0	0	1	3	1	.071	.071	5	**20**	**1**
Frank Baker	3b	4	16	0	4	2	0	0	2	1	3	0	.250	.375	10	15	0
Eddie Murphy	rf	4	16	2	3	2	0	0	0	2	2	0	.188	.313	4	0	0
Amos Strunk	cf	2	7	0	2	0	0	0	0	0	2	0	.286	.286	4	0	0
Rube Oldring	lf	4	15	0	1	0	0	0	0	0	**5**	0	.067	.067	6	0	0
Wally Schang	c	4	12	1	2	1	0	0	0	1	4	0	.167	.250	17	3	**1**
Jimmy Walsh	ph-cf	3	6	0	2	1	0	0	1	3	1	0	.333	.500	2	0	0
Jack Lapp	c	1	1	0	0	0	0	0	0	0	0	0	.000	.000	2	1	0
Larry Kopf		Did not play															
Chick Davies		Did not play															
Shag Thompson		Did not play															
Wickey McAvoy		Did not play															
Harry Davis		Did not play															
Ira Thomas		Did not play															
Bullet Joe Bush	p	1	5	0	0	0	0	0	0	0	2	0	.000	.000	0	5	**1**
Eddie Plank	p	1	2	0	0	0	0	0	0	0	1	0	.000	.000	0	1	0
Chief Bender	p	1	2	0	0	0	0	0	0	0	0	0	.000	.000	1	3	0
Bob Shawkey	p	1	2	0	1	1	0	0	1	0	1	0	.500	1.000	0	3	0
Weldon Wyckoff	p	1	1	0	1	1	0	0	0	0	0	0	1.000	2.000	1	0	0
Herb Pennock	p	1	1	0	0	0	0	0	0	0	0	0	.000	.000	0	0	0
Rube Bressler		Did not play															
Jack Coombs		Did not play															
team total		4	128	6	22	9	0	0	5	13	28	2	.172	.242	111	65	4

Double Plays—4
Left on Bases—21

REGULAR SEASON STATISTICS

PHILADELPHIA ATHLETICS		Main Pos	G	AB	R	H	2B	3B	HR	RBI	BB	SO	SB	BA	SA
Stuffy McInnis		1b	149	576	74	181	12	8	1	95	19	27	25	.314	.368
Eddie Collins		2b	152	526	**122**	181	23	14	2	85	97	31	58	.344	.452
Jack Barry		ss	140	467	57	113	12	0	0	42	53	34	22	.242	.268
Frank Baker		3b	150	570	84	182	23	10	**9**	89	53	37	19	.319	.442
Eddie Murphy		of	148	573	101	156	12	9	3	43	87	46	36	.272	.340
Amos Strunk		of	122	404	58	111	15	3	2	45	57	38	25	.275	.342
Rube Oldring		of	119	466	68	129	21	7	3	49	18	35	14	.277	.371
Wally Schang		c	107	307	44	88	11	8	3	45	32	33	7	.287	.404
Jimmy Walsh	f	of	67	216	35	51	11	6	3	36	30	27	6	.236	.384
Jack Lapp		c	69	199	22	46	7	2	0	19	31	14	1	.231	.286
Larry Kopf		ss-3b-2b	35	69	8	13	2	2	0	12	8	14	6	.188	.275
Chick Davies		of-p	19	46	6	11	3	1	0	5	5	13	1	.239	.348
Shag Thompson		of	16	29	3	5	0	1	0	2	7	8	1	172	.241
Wickey McAvoy		c	18	16	1	2	0	1	0	0	0	4	0	.125	.250
Harry Davis		1b	5	7	0	3	0	0	0	2	1	0	0	.429	.429
Ira Thomas		c	2	3	0	0	0	0	0	0	0	0	0	.000	.000
Bullet Joe Bush		p	38	74	6	14	4	0	1	8	2	25	0	.189	.284
Eddie Plank		p	34	60	6	9	2	0	0	5	4	14	1	.150	.183
Chief Bender		p	28	62	4	9	1	0	1	8	4	13	0	.145	.210
Bob Shawkey		p	38	83	6	17	2	0	0	5	4	22	0	.205	.229
Weldon Wyckoff		p	34	75	7	11	0	0	1	6	4	15	3	.147	.187
Herb Pennock		p	28	56	7	12	0	2	0	9	2	11	0	.214	.286
Rube Bressler		p	29	51	6	11	1	1	0	4	6	7	0	.216	.275
Jack Coombs		p-of	5	11	0	3	1	0	0	2	1	1	0	.273	.364
team total			157	5126	**749**	**392**	165	80	**29**	**627**	545	512	231	**.272**	**.352**

f—from New York (A)
John Coyle (3b), Sam Crane (ss), Press Cruthers (2b), Tom Daley (of), Earle Mack (1b), Ferdie Moore (1b), Bill Orr (ss), Ben Rochefort (1b), Dean Sturgis (c), Charlie Sweeney (of), Charlie Boardman (p), Boardwalk Brown (p), Duke Houck (p), Bill Jensen (p), Fred Worden (p), also played for the Athletics during the season.

PITCHING

WORLD SERIES STATISTICS

	G	GS	CG	IP	H	R	ER	BB	SO	W	L	SV	ERA
BOSTON BRAVES													
Dick Rudolph	**2**	**2**	**2**	**18**	**12**	2	1	4	**15**	**2**	0	0	0.50
Bill James	**2**	1	1	11	2	0	0	**6**	9	**2**	0	0	**0.00**
Letty Tyler	1	1	0	10	8	4	4	3	4	0	0	0	3.60
Dick Crutcher	Did not play												
Otto Hess	Did not play												
George Davis	Did not play												
Paul Strand	Did not play												
Gene Cocreham	Did not play												
Dick Cottrell	Did not play												
team total	4	4	3	39	22	6	5	13	28	4	0	0	1.15
PHILADELPHIA ATHLETICS													
Bullet Joe Bush	1	1	1	11	9	5	4	4	4	0	**1**	0	3.27
Eddie Plank	1	1	1	9	7	1	1	4	6	0	**1**	0	1.00
Chief Bender	1	1	0	5⅓	8	**6**	**6**	2	3	0	**1**	0	10.13
Bob Shawkey	1	1	0	5	4	3	2	2	0	0	**1**	0	3.60
Weldon Wyckoff	1	0	0	3⅔	3	1	1	1	2	0	0	0	2.45
Herb Pennock	1	0	0	3	2	0	0	2	3	0	0	0	0.00
Rube Bressler	Did not play												
Chick Davies	Did not play												
Jack Coombs	Did not play												
team total	4	4	2	37	33	16	14	15	18	0	4	0	3.41

REGULAR SEASON STATISTICS

	G	GS	CG	IP	H	ER	BB	SO	W	L	Pct	SV	ShO	ERA
BOSTON BRAVES														
Dick Rudolph	42	36	31	336	288	88	61	138	**27**	10	.730	0	6	2.36
Bill James	46	37	30	332	261	70	118	156	26	7	**.788**	2	4	1.90
Letty Tyler	38	34	21	271	247	81	101	140	16	14	.533	2	5	2.69
Dick Crutcher	33	15	5	159	169	61	66	48	5	6	.455	0	1	3.45
Otto Hess	14	11	7	89	89	30	33	24	5	6	.455	1	1	3.03
George Davis	9	6	4	56	42	21	26	26	3	3	.500	0	1	3.38
Paul Strand	16	3	1	55	47	15	23	33	6	2	.750	0	0	2.45
Gene Cocreham	15	3	1	45	48	24	27	15	3	4	.429	0	0	4.80
Dick Cottrell	1	1	0	1	2	1	3	1	0	1	.000	0	0	9.00
team total	158	158	**104**	1421	1272	433	477	606	**94**	59	**.614**	5	18	2.74
PHILADELPHIA ATHLETICS														
Bullet Joe Bush	38	22	14	206	184	70	81	109	17	12	.586	2	2	3.06
Eddie Plank	34	22	11	185	178	59	42	110	15	7	.682	2	4	2.87
Chief Bender	28	23	14	179	159	45	55	107	17	3	**.850**	0	7	2.26
Bob Shawkey	38	31	18	237	223	72	75	89	16	8	.667	2	5	2.73
Weldon Wyckoff	32	20	11	185	153	62	103	86	11	8	.579	2	0	3.02
Herb Pennock	28	14	8	152	136	47	65	90	11	4	.733	3	3	2.78
Rube Bressler	29	10	8	148	112	29	56	96	10	3	.769	2	1	1.76
Chick Davies	1	1	1	9	8	1	3	4	1	0	1.000	0	0	1.00
Jack Coombs	2	2	0	8	8	4	3	1	0	1	.000	0	0	4.50
team total	157	157	88	1404	1264	433	521	720	**99**	53	**.651**	13	22	2.78

Total Attendance—111,009 Average Attendance—27,752 Winning Player's Share—$2,812 Losing Player's Share—$2,032

1914

Boston Braves vs. Philadelphia Athletics

On June 28, 1914, a shot rang out in Sarajevo that would change the world. Archduke Francis Ferdinand, heir to the Austrian throne, lay dead, the victim of an assassin. World War I was imminent as entente followed entente into war. The world no longer would be the same.

But while the world was changing, the world of baseball remained remarkably constant. For on that day in June, the Boston Braves were residing in their familiar position—last place. Throughout their short fourteen-year history, the Braves had compiled baseball's sorriest record: only one winning season and an average won-lost record of 58 wins and 90 losses, finishing last five times and losing more than 100 games on six separate occasions. The year 1914 appeared to be no different.

However, 1914 was to be different. Much different. It was to become the year of the "Miracle Braves," a ragtag group of players who managed to bring off what the Associated Press, in its half-century poll, would later vote to be the "Upset of the Twentieth Century."

Perhaps their transformation from perennial losers into "Miracle Braves" began with the appointment of George Tweedy Stallings as manager before the 1913 season. Stallings, together with his widely respected coach, Fred Mitchell, took the Braves from last place in 1912 to a respectable fifth-place finish in '13, their highest position in the final standings since 1902.

Stallings was a man deeply dedicated to winning, and he instilled in his troops a philosophy similar to that of Knute Rockne: the team that won't be beaten can't be beaten. Stallings tolerated no less than total commitment; slackers soon found themselves not only off his starting lineup, but off his team as well. He mixed this total dedication with more than a small pinch of sarcasm. On one occasion he watched in horror as two players, newly arrived from college campuses, committed base-running blunders that ended with their both being caught in rundowns for an inning-ending double play. Stallings stuck his face in theirs, and in the staccato bark of a cheerleader bellowed, "Rah, rah, rah! Rah, rah, rah!"

But Stallings was only half the story. The other half was the addition the Braves made in February, 1914, when they picked up Johnny Evers, the little pepper-pot second baseman who had been released two months before by the Chicago Cubs. Evers, immortalized by Franklin P. Adams as one of the "trio of bear Cubs fleeter than birds," had been a winner for most of his 12-year career, having never played full-time for a team that had finished below third. But after managing the Cubs to a third-place finish in 1913—a year in which he, not incidentally, hit .284 in 135 games, higher than any returning Brave—he was dismissed by the Cub management, both as a

manager and as a player. And so Stallings picked up the man who had been described in his original scouting report as being "about the size of a double-jointed peanut, with a little, old-looking face," as his second baseman, and second manager. Together, they would forge the "Miracle Braves" out of the nine-man sow's ear that took the field on opening day.

The Braves hardly looked like a potential pennant winner. They were a bunch of have-nots and never-wases, not even household names in their own houses—with the exception of Evers. The first baseman was Butch Schmidt, who described himself as "the best first baseman in the world." And yet Schmidt had accumulated the somewhat less than sterling total of 24 hits in two years of part-time play. Charlie Deal, the third baseman, had just 54 hits in two years. Shortstop Walter Maranville—known as "Rabbit," he would become known by National League fans over the next two decades for his circus vest-pocket catches of towering flies and his ability to drink—had just 159 hits in two years, and catcher Hank Gowdy, 61 in four. If you add rookie outfielder Larry Gilbert, outfielder Les Man, going into his second year, outfielder Joe Connolly, also a sophomore, and utility man Possum Whitted, the starting lineup for the 1914 Braves—excluding Evers—had amassed the magnificent total of 612 hits in big-league play. Hardly the makings of a miracle team.

The pitching staff appeared to be no better: "Seattle" Bill James, a second-year man, had a 6–10 lifetime record; spitballer Dick Rudolph had compiled a 14–14 record in three years; Lefty Tyler, a 34–49 record. The remainder of the staff numbered six. Of these, two were rookies and none of the rest had winning lifetime records. No potential pennant winner, or pennant contender, for that matter, had such a losing staff.

It was no surprise, then, to find the Braves in last place on June 28. Or on July 4, for that matter, 15 games behind the front-running New York Giants. By July 19, they had closed the gap to 11 games, but still found themselves in their usual position, ever the National League cellar.

Then, in a dog-bites-man type of story, the Boston Braves won 12 games. They followed this up by winning a doubleheader from the Reds, moving into seventh place, ahead of the Pirates, and by the afternoon of July 21 found themselves in the heady position of fourth place. They followed that with nine straight wins and passed Chicago to move into third, and within three weeks had moved into second place.

With manager Stallings wearing out the seat of his civilian tweeds by constant twitchings, and flashing signals by baring his pearly whites, the pitching staff putting together pitching jewel after pitching jewel, and the rest of the team scratching and clawing its way to miracle finish after miracle finish, the Braves tied for the lead by Labor Day. Two days later they went ahead for good in a showdown, and soon turned the dog-fight into a runaway, winning the pennant by 10½ games.

Although their sudden transformation from doormat to flying carpet was due in part to the late-season acquisition of two players—third baseman "Red" Smith and outfielder Josh Devore—the primary reason for their rush to the top was their pitching staff. From mid-July on, Bill James won 19 of his last 20 decisions, Dick Rudolph put together a 12-game winning streak and Lefty Tyler tossed in at least a dozen well-pitched games.

The scriptwriter for the then-popular "Perils of Pauline" could not have concocted a wilder or wackier scenario than the Braves put together in 1914. With Rudolph, James and Tyler winning a total of 69 of the team's 94 victories, one would have thought there was little room for any other member of the pitching staff. Wrong! On September 9, young George Davis, a Harvard Law School student, threw the National League's only no-hitter of the season, moving the Braves into first place—permanently. Then, on September 29, Tom Hughes won his only game of the season, the pennant clincher. It was that kind of a year for the "Miracle Braves"—last in the league in stolen bases, sixth in bases on balls given up, fifth in slugging average and strikeouts pitched, fourth in ERA and batting average, third in home runs and first in the National League!

But still, even the most foolhardy, even those who believe in good fairies, would never have scripted what happened next. For it was believed, by almost all observers, that the team which had won the National League pennant in a breeze and captured the imagination of the nation in the process would run out of miracles when it came to the World Series.

Their opponents were the mighty Philadelphia A's, the proud possessors of the mantle "World's Champions" three times in the past four years, and rarely extended in their fight to retain that crown—losing only four games in those three Series. These were the A's of the $100,000 infield—McInnis, Collins, Barry and Baker. They had a pitching staff that numbered among its members future Hall of Famers Eddie Plank, Chief Bender, Jack Coombs and Herb Pennock, together with second bananas like Bob Shawkey, "Bullet" Joe Bush and Rube Bressler. These were Connie Mack's "White Elephants," winners of 583 games over the past six years—an average of 97 games a year. What chance did the Braves, miracle or no, stand against them? Few, if any, gave them a chance.

But if America lacked confidence in the Braves, the Braves more than made up for it all by themselves. When Harry Davis, the venerable captain of the A's, visited the Polo Grounds to scout his team's opponent in the Series, he chanced to meet the diminutive Braves outfielder Herbie Moran, another late-season acquisition in Stallings' rotating player lineup. "You fellows did a great job, Herbie," said the A's captain, "and I expect we'll have a great Series." "Harry," answered little Herbie, drawing his five-foot, five-inch frame up to his pouter-pigeon fullest, "I don't think you fellows will win a single game."

And damned if Moran wasn't right! Even without their starting third baseman, J. Carlisle "Red" Smith—who broke his leg on the last day of the season—the Braves out-hit, out-hustled and simply outplayed the A's on every level, doing what they had done all year, winning. Behind only once in the four games, they relied on the magic of their three-man pitching staff, with James and Rudolph winning two games each, to beat the A's in four straight.

With Chief Bender—the American League's leading pitcher, with a 17-3 record—going for the A's, and Rudolph going for the Braves, the Series opened in Philadelphia on October 9. It began to look like the critics were right when the Braves went out 1-2-3 in the first inning, and the first Philadelphia batter, Eddie Murphy, singled to center off Rudolph. But in the second the Braves put together a walk, a double by Hank Gowdy and a single by Maranville to take a 2-0 lead, one they would never relinquish as Rudolph spaced four other hits over the next eight innings to come away a winner, 5-1. The second game was more of the same, with the bats of the A's suddenly very quiet, and James winning on a two-hitter, 1-0.

So supremely confident were the Braves, now up two games to none, that, upon their arrival back in Boston, they refused to pack their bags for a potential return trip to Philadelphia for games five and six.

Game three saw the A's take the lead for the first time in the Series with a run in the first, but the Braves tied it in the second. Philadelphia went ahead again in the fourth with another run, and once again the Braves tied it in their half of the inning. It remained deadlocked 2-2 through nine innings, with Tyler and "Bullet" Joe Bush both hurling six-hitters. In the top of the tenth, the A's went ahead for the third time in the game—and the Series—with two runs off Tyler. But in the bottom of the tenth, Hank Gowdy hit the only homer of the Series and the Braves scratched back, as they had done all year, to tie it up again. Finally, with Dick James pitching, the Braves put together another Gowdy extra-base hit—his fifth of the Series, setting records for slugging average with 1.273, and a four-game batting average with .545—to win the game 5-4.

That was to be the A's last gasp as Rudolph wound it up the next afternoon before an overflow crowd at Fenway Park, borrowed from the Red Sox for the occasion, with a 3-1 win. Evers fittingly drove in the Braves' winning runs.

The "Miracle Braves" had brought if off; they had held the mighty A's in check to win four straight games, the first time this had been done in World Series history. And their pitching staff, ridiculed before the season, had held the mighty A's to just 22 hits and a .172 team batting average, the lowest in World Series history. It was baseball's version of a fairy tale, a miracle which no one had believed could happen—no one except George Stallings and the "Miracle Braves."

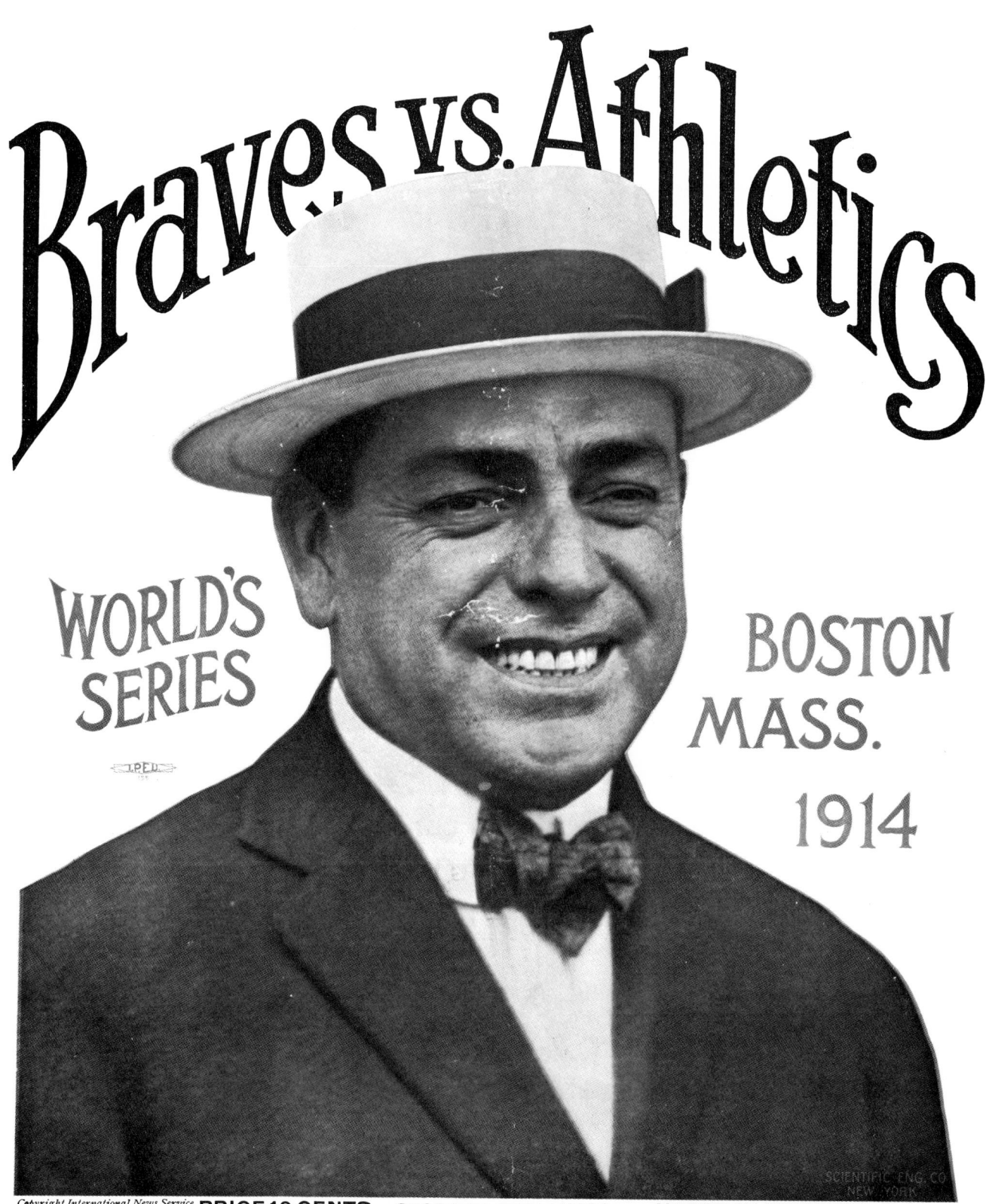

Braves vs. Athletics

WORLD'S SERIES

BOSTON MASS.

1914

PRICE 10 CENTS   GEORGE T. STALLINGS
(THE MIRACLE MAN)   HARRY M. STEVENS, Publisher

JAMES E. GAFFNEY
President Boston National League Club

FREDERICK R. KILLEEN
Assistant Treasurer Boston National League Ball Club

HERMAN NICKERSON
Secretary Boston National League Club

J. J. LANNIN
President Boston American League Club

The gentleman who so kindly made it possible to accommodate the increasing
attendance by loaning his grounds to our Club. I wish to take this opportunity
to thank him publicly for all the courtesies our Club has received at his hands.
Statement of President Gaffney.

GEORGE T. STALLINGS   JAMES E. GAFFNEY   JOHN EVERS

Copyright W. W. Somers   RUDOLPH   JAMES   TYLER
                                THE BIG THREE

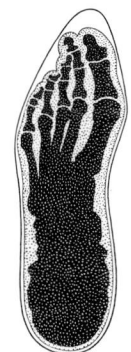
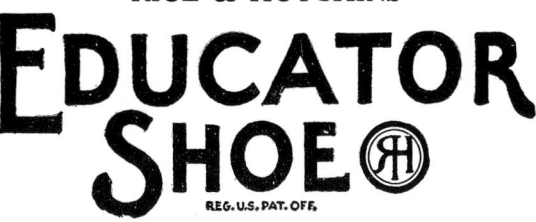
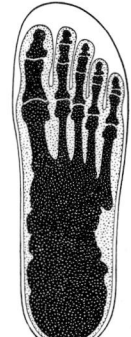

17. Davis	18. Strand	22. Cocreham	23. Cottrell										
51. Gilbert	71. Dugey	149. Mitchell											

BOSTON

	1	2	3	4	5	6	7	8	9	10	AB	R	1B	S.H	P.O	A	E
1. Moran / 61. Mann r. f.	◇	◇	◇	◇	◇	◇	◇	◇	◇	◇							
2. Evers 2 b.	◇	◇	◇	◇	◇	◇	◇	◇	◇	◇							
3. Connolly / 24. Cather l. f.	◇	◇	◇	◇	◇	◇	◇	◇	◇	◇							
4. Whitted / 49. Devore c. f.	◇	◇	◇	◇	◇	◇	◇	◇	◇	◇							
5. Schmidt 1 b.	◇	◇	◇	◇	◇	◇	◇	◇	◇	◇							
6. Smith / 112. Deal 3 b.	◇	◇	◇	◇	◇	◇	◇	◇	◇	◇							
7. Maranville s. s.	◇	◇	◇	◇	◇	◇	◇	◇	◇	◇							
8. Gowdy / 9. Whaling c.	◇	◇	◇	◇	◇	◇	◇	◇	◇	◇							
11. Tyler / 12. Rudolph / 14. Hess / 15. James / 16. Crutcher p.	◇	◇	◇	◇	◇	◇	◇	◇	◇	◇							

UMPIRES
30. Klem   31. Byron—N.L.
32. Dineen 33. Hildebrand—A.L.

Earned Runs........Two-Base Hits..........Three-Base Hits........Home Runs........Passed Balls........Wild Pitches........

Bases on Balls........Bases on Hit by Pitched Ball........Struck Out........Left on Bases........Double Plays........Time........

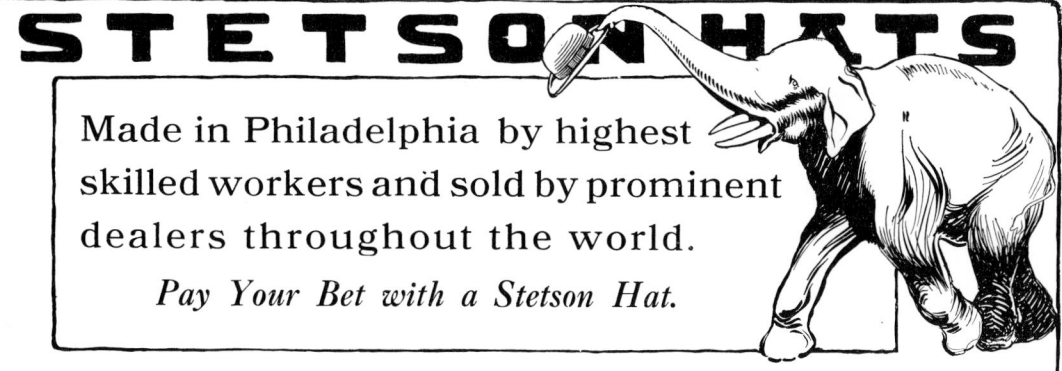

17. Pennock	19. Coombs	21. Walsh	23. Davis	25. Davies
18. Kopf	20. Wyckoff	22. McAvoy	24. Thompson	

PHILADELPHIA

		1	2	3	4	5	6	7	8	9	10	AB	R	1B	SH	P.O	A	E
1. Murphy	r. f.																	
2. Oldring	l. f.																	
3. Collins	2 b.																	
4. Baker	3 b.																	
5. McInnis	1 b.																	
6. Strunk	c. f.																	
7. Barry	s. s.																	
8. Schang 9. Lapp 10. Thomas	c.																	
11. Bender 12. Plank 14. Bush 15. Shawkey 16. Bressler	p.																	

UMPIRES
30. Klem   31. Byron—N.L.
32. Dineen 33. Hildebrand—A.L.

Earned Runs........Two-Base Hits........Three-Base Hits........Home Runs........Passed Balls........Wild Pitches........

Bases on Balls........Bases on Hit by Pitched Ball........Struck Out........Left on Bases........Double Plays........Time........

PUREOXIA

GINGER ALE

MADE WITH DISTILLED WATER

BOSTON "BRAVES," CHAMPIONS NATIONAL LEAGUE, 1914

Copyright W. W. Somers, 1914

Top Row—James, Cather, Deal, Davis, Cottrell, Cocreham, Hess, Mann, Gowdy, Schmidt, Whaling
Centre Row—Whitted, Dugey, Tyler, Strand, Devore, Gilbert, Smith, Moran
Bottom Row—Connolly, Mitchell, Young Connolly (mascot), Rudolph, Maranville, Crutcher, Martin, Evers

CLARK GRIFFITH AND PRESIDENT JAMES E. GAFFNEY
Manager
Washington Baseball Club
The man who was the first to interest Mr. Gaffney in Baseball

Mr. CORNELIUS McGILLICUDDY
"Connie Mack," Manager Philadelphia Athletics

PHILADELPHIA ATHLETICS, CHAMPIONS AMERICAN LEAGUE, 1914.

Top Row—Plank, Davis, Houck, Baker, Thomas, Brown, Bender, Wyckoff, Pennock
Centre Row—Strunk, Lapp, Daley, Schang, Bush, Connie Mack, D. Murphy, Shawkey, Orr, Oldring
Bottom Row—Walsh, Lavan, Barry, E. Murphy, Collins, McInnis

THE BOSTON SCRIBES

Top Row, Left to Right—Edward T. McGrath, *Boston Post;* A. H. C. Mitchell, *American;* J. C. O'Leary, *Globe;* Fred. J. Hoey, *American;* William Swan, *Asso. Press;* Burt Whitman, *Herald.* Centre Row, Left to Right—W. E. Hapgood, *Herald;* T. H. Murnane, *Globe;* R. E. McMillan, *Journal;* P. E. Harrison, *N. Y. Sun;* M. E. Webb, Jr., *Globe.* Bottom Row, Left to Right—N. Flatley, *American;* J. W. Moran, Jr., *Journal;* George Carens, *Boston Transcript*

AUGUST HERMANN
President National Committee

The National Commission

JOHN K. TENER
President National League

B. B. JOHNSON
President American League

 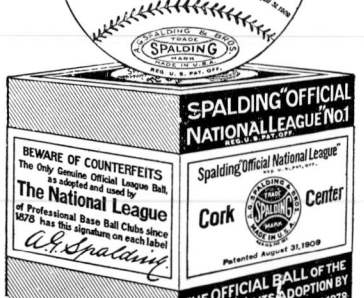 

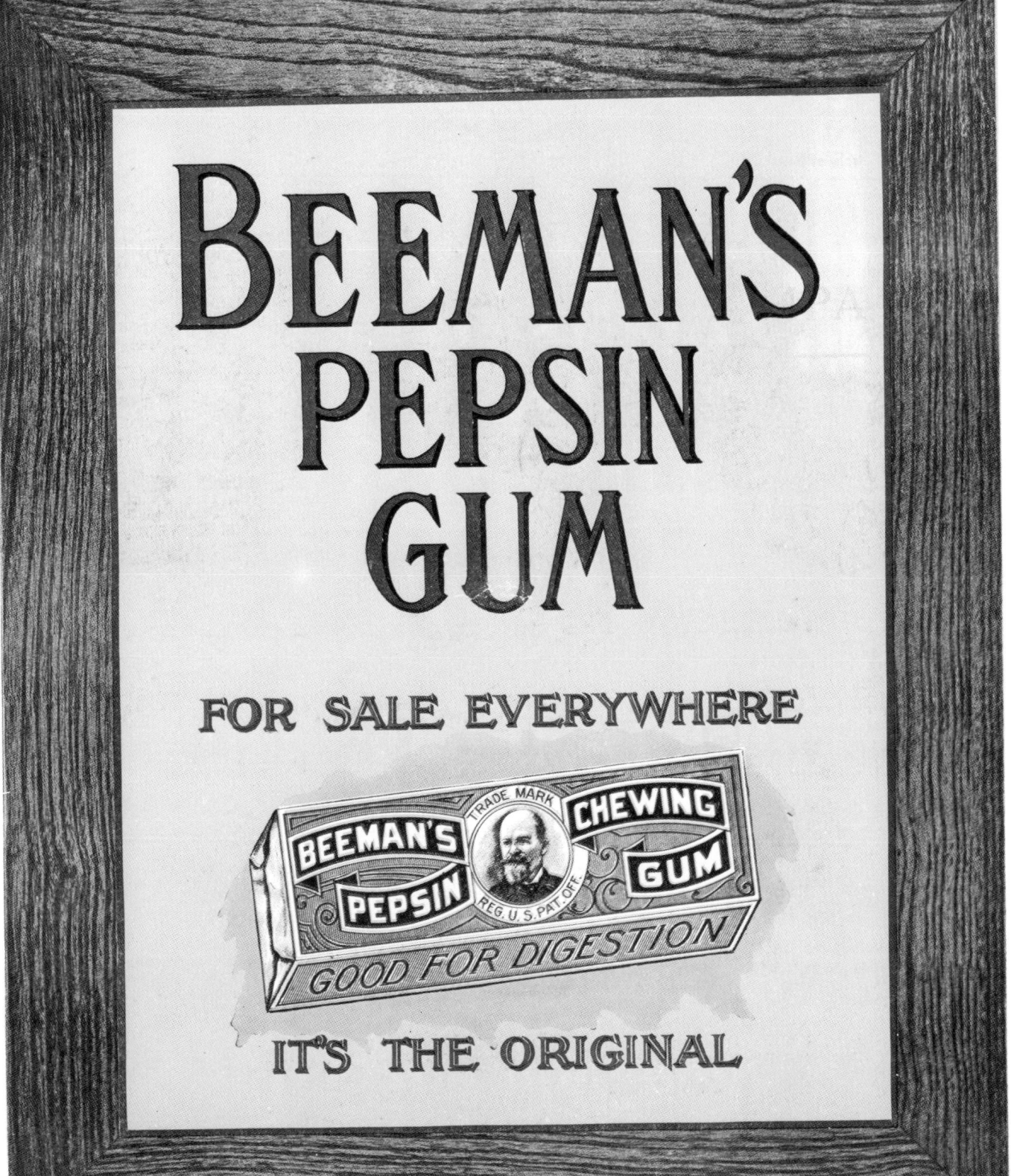

1917

Chicago White Sox
vs.
New York Giants

1917 WORLD SERIES COMPOSITE BOX

	Wins	Composite Line Score
Chicago White Sox (A.L.)	4	0 2 2 9 0 1 3 3 1 – 21
New York Giants (N.L.)	2	2 2 0 5 4 0 2 2 0 – 17

Manager	W	L	Pct.	G. Ahead
	Regular Season			
Pants Rowland	100	54	.649	9
John McGraw	98	56	.636	10

BATTING AND FIELDING

CHICAGO WHITE SOX

WORLD SERIES STATISTICS

	Pos	G	AB	R	H	2B	3B	HR	RBI	BB	SO	SB	BA	SA	PO	A	E
Chick Gandil	1b	6	23	1	6	1	0	0	5	0	2	1	.261	.304	67	3	1
Eddie Collins	2b	6	22	4	9	1	0	0	2	2	3	3	.409	.455	11	23	0
Buck Weaver	ss	6	21	3	7	1	0	0	1	0	2	0	.333	.381	13	14	4
Fred McMullin	3b	6	24	1	3	1	0	0	2	1	6	0	.125	.167	2	14	0
Shano Collins	rf	6	21	2	6	1	0	0	0	0	2	0	.286	.333	4	1	3
Happy Felsch	cf	6	22	4	6	1	0	1	3	1	5	0	.273	.455	16	2	0
Joe Jackson	lf	6	23	4	7	0	0	0	2	1	0	1	.304	.304	9	1	0
Ray Schalk	c	6	19	1	5	0	0	0	0	2	1	1	.263	.263	32	6	2
Nemo Leibold	ph-rf	2	5	1	2	0	0	0	2	1	1	0	.400	.400	1	0	0
Swede Risberg	ph	2	2	0	1	0	0	0	1	0	0	0	.500	.500			
Byrd Lynn	ph	1	1	0	0	0	0	0	0	0	1	0	.000	.000			
Eddie Murphy		Did not play															
Ted Jourdan		Did not play															
Joe Jenkins		Did not play															
Ziggy Hasbrouck		Did not play															
Bobby Byrne		Did not play															
Red Faber	p	4	7	0	1	0	0	0	0	2	3	0	.143	.143	1	9	0
Eddie Cicotte	p	3	7	0	1	0	0	0	0	1	2	0	.143	.143	0	6	1
Lefty Williams	p	1	0	0	0	0	0	0	0	0	0	0	—	—	0	0	1
Dave Danforth	p	1	0	0	0	0	0	0	0	0	0	0	—	—	0	1	0
Reb Russell	p	1	0	0	0	0	0	0	0	0	0	0	—	—	0	0	0
Jim Scott		Did not play															
Joe Benz		Did not play															
Mellie Wolfgang		Did not play															
team total		6	197	21	54	6	0	1	18	11	28	6	.274	.315	156	79	12

Double Plays—6
Left on Bases—39

REGULAR SEASON STATISTICS

	Main Pos	G	AB	R	H	2B	3B	HR	RBI	BB	SO	SB	BA	SA
Chick Gandil	1b	149	553	53	151	9	7	0	57	30	36	16	.273	.315
Eddie Collins	2b	156	564	91	163	18	12	0	67	89	16	53	.289	.363
Buck Weaver	3b	118	447	64	127	16	5	3	32	27	29	19	.284	.362
Fred McMullin	3b	59	194	35	46	2	1	0	12	27	17	9	.237	.258
Shano Collins	of	82	252	38	59	13	3	1	14	10	27	14	.234	.321
Happy Felsch	of	152	575	75	177	17	10	6	102	33	52	26	.308	.403
Joe Jackson	of	146	538	91	162	20	17	5	75	57	25	13	.301	.429
Ray Schalk	c	140	424	48	96	12	5	2	51	59	27	19	.226	.292
Nemo Leibold	of	125	428	59	101	12	6	0	29	74	34	27	.236	.292
Swede Risberg	ss	149	474	59	96	20	8	1	45	59	65	16	.203	.285
Byrd Lynn	c	35	72	7	16	2	0	0	5	7	11	1	.222	.250
Eddie Murphy	of	53	51	9	16	2	1	0	16	5	1	4	.314	.392
Ted Jourdan	1b	17	34	2	5	0	1	0	2	1	3	0	.147	.206
Joe Jenkins	ph	10	9	0	1	0	0	0	2	0	5	0	.111	.111
Ziggy Hasbrouck	2b	2	1	1	0	0	0	0	0	0	0	0	.000	.000
Bobby Byrne	a 2b	1	1	0	0	0	0	0	0	0	0	0	.000	.000
Red Faber	p	41	69	1	4	1	0	0	2	10	38	0	.058	.072
Eddie Cicotte	p	49	112	6	20	2	0	0	8	12	23	1	.179	.196
Lefty Williams	p	45	67	5	6	0	1	0	2	8	19	0	.090	.119
Dave Danforth	p	50	46	3	6	2	1	0	5	6	19	1	.130	.217
Reb Russell	p	39	68	5	19	3	3	0	9	2	10	0	.279	.412
Jim Scott	p	24	42	1	5	0	0	0	0	4	9	0	.119	.119
Joe Benz	p	19	30	4	5	1	0	0	0	0	11	0	.167	.200
Mellie Wolfgang	p	5	4	0	0	0	0	0	0	0	1	0	.000	.000
team total		156	5057	657	1281	152	81	18	535	522	479	219	.253	.326

a—from Philadelphia (N)
Jack Fournier (ph). Zeb Terry (ss) also played for the White Sox during the season.

NEW YORK GIANTS

WORLD SERIES STATISTICS

	Pos	G	AB	R	H	2B	3B	HR	RBI	BB	SO	SB	BA	SA	PO	A	E
Walter Holke	1b	6	21	2	6	2	0	0	1	0	6	0	.286	.381	67	0	1
Buck Herzog	2b	6	24	1	6	0	1	0	2	1	4	0	.250	.333	11	12	2
Art Fletcher	ss	6	25	2	5	1	0	0	0	0	2	0	.200	.240	9	17	3
Heinie Zimmerman	3b	6	25	1	3	0	1	0	0	0	0	0	.120	.200	9	14	2
Dave Robertson	rf	6	22	3	11	1	1	0	1	0	0	2	.500	.636	6	2	1
Benny Kauff	cf	6	25	2	4	1	0	2	5	0	2	1	.160	.440	6	0	1
George Burns	lf	6	22	3	5	0	0	0	2	2	6	1	.227	.227	11	0	0
Bill Rariden	c	5	13	2	5	0	0	0	2	2	1	0	.385	.385	25	10	0
Lew McCarty	c-ph	3	5	1	2	0	1	0	1	0	0	0	.400	.800	7	1	1
Joe Wilhoit	ph	2	1	0	0	0	0	0	0	1	0	0	.000	.000			
Jim Thorpe	rf	1	0	0	0	0	0	0	0	0	0	0	—	—	0	0	0
Jimmy Smith		Did not play															
George Gibson		Did not play															
Hans Lobert		Did not play															
Al Baird		Did not play															
Red Murray		Did not play															
Jack Onslow		Did not play															
Slim Sallee	p	2	6	0	1	0	0	0	1	0	2	0	.167	.167	0	8	0
Rube Benton	p	2	4	0	0	0	0	0	0	0	3	0	.000	.000	1	2	0
Ferdie Schupp	p	2	4	0	1	0	0	0	1	0	1	0	.250	.250	1	4	0
Pol Perritt	p	3	2	0	2	0	0	0	0	0	0	0	1.000	1.000	0	1	0
Fred Anderson	p	1	0	0	0	0	0	0	0	0	0	0	—	—	0	1	0
Jeff Tesreau	p	1	0	0	0	0	0	0	0	0	0	0	—	—	0	0	0
Al Demaree		Did not play															
team total		6	199	17	51	5	4	2	16	6	27	4	.256	.352	153	72	1

Double Plays—3
Left on Bases—37

REGULAR SEASON STATISTICS

	Main Pos	G	AB	R	H	2B	3B	HR	RBI	BB	SO	SB	BA	SA
Walter Holke	1b	153	527	55	146	12	7	2	55	34	54	13	.277	.338
Buck Herzog	2b	114	417	69	98	10	8	2	31	31	36	12	.235	.312
Art Fletcher	ss	151	557	70	145	24	5	4	56	23	28	12	.260	.343
Heinie Zimmerman	3b	150	585	61	174	22	9	5	102	16	43	13	.297	.391
Dave Robertson	of	142	532	64	138	16	9	12	54	10	47	17	.259	.391
Benny Kauff	of	153	559	89	172	22	4	5	68	59	54	30	.308	.388
George Burns	of	152	597	103	180	25	13	5	45	75	55	40	.302	.412
Bill Rariden	c	101	266	20	72	10	1	0	25	42	17	3	.271	.316
Lew McCarty	c	56	162	15	40	3	2	2	19	14	6	1	.247	.327
Joe Wilhoit	of	34	50	9	17	2	2	0	8	8	5	0	.340	.460
Jim Thorpe	b of	26	57	12	11	3	2	0	4	8	10	1	.193	.316
Jimmy Smith	2b	36	96	12	22	5	1	0	2	9	18	6	.229	.302
George Gibson	c	35	82	1	14	3	0	0	5	7	2	1	.171	.207
Hans Lobert	3b	35	52	4	10	1	0	1	5	5	5	2	.192	.269
Al Baird	2b-ss	18	24	1	7	0	0	0	4	2	2	2	.292	.292
Red Murray	of	22	22	1	1	1	0	0	3	4	3	0	.045	.091
Jack Onslow	c	9	8	1	2	1	0	0	0	0	1	0	.250	.375
Slim Sallee	p	34	77	7	17	0	0	0	11	2	12	0	.221	.221
Rube Benton	p	35	72	1	12	1	1	0	2	2	18	0	.167	.208
Ferdie Schupp	p	36	93	6	15	2	1	0	4	8	35	0	.161	.204
Pol Perritt	p	35	70	4	11	1	0	0	3	0	20	0	.157	.171
Fred Anderson	p	38	42	2	3	0	0	0	1	3	14	0	.071	.071
Jeff Tesreau	p	33	61	4	14	0	1	0	5	1	9	1	.230	.262
Al Demaree	c p	15	18	2	2	0	0	0	2	1	6	1	.111	.111
team total		158	5211	635	1360	170	71	39	537	373	533	162	.261	.343

b—from Cincinnati
c—from Chicago (A)
Ed Hemingway (3b), Pete Kilduff (2b), Ernie Krueger (c), Joe Rodriguez (1b), Ross Youngs (of), George Kelly (p), Jim Middleton (p), George Smith (p), Ad Swigler (p) also played for the Giants during the season.

PITCHING

CHICAGO WHITE SOX

WORLD SERIES STATISTICS

	G	GS	CG	IP	H	R	ER	BB	SO	W	L	SV	ERA
Red Faber	4	3	2	27	21	7	7	3	9	3	1	0	2.33
Eddie Cicotte	3	2	2	23	23	6	5	2	13	1	1	0	1.95
Lefty Williams	1	0	0	1	2	1	1	0	3	0	0	0	9.00
Dave Danforth	1	0	0	1	3	2	2	0	2	0	0	0	18.00
Reb Russell	1	1	0	0	2	1	1	1	0	0	0	0	∞
Jim Scott	Did not play												
Joe Benz	Did not play												
Mellie Wolfgang	Did not play												
team total	6	6	4	52	51	17	16	6	27	4	2	0	2.77

REGULAR SEASON STATISTICS

	G	GS	CG	IP	H	ER	BB	SO	W	L	Pct	SV	ShO	ERA
Red Faber	41	29	17	248	224	53	85	84	16	13	.552	3	3	1.92
Eddie Cicotte	49	35	29	347	246	59	70	150	28	12	.700	4	7	1.53
Lefty Williams	45	29	8	230	221	76	81	85	11	8	.680	1	1	2.47
Dave Danforth	50	9	1	173	155	51	74	79	11	6	.647	11	1	2.65
Reb Russell	35	24	11	189	170	41	32	54	15	5	.750	4	5	1.95
Jim Scott	24	17	6	125	126	26	42	37	6	7	.462	0	2	1.87
Joe Benz	19	13	7	95	76	26	23	25	7	3	.700	0	2	2.46
Mellie Wolfgang	5	0	0	18	18	10	6	3	0	0	—	0	0	5.00
team total	156	156	79	1424	1236	342	413	517	100	54	.649	23	21	2.16

NEW YORK GIANTS

WORLD SERIES STATISTICS

	G	GS	CG	IP	H	R	ER	BB	SO	W	L	SV	ERA
Slim Sallee	2	2	1	15 1/3	20	10	9	4	4	0	2	0	5.28
Rube Benton	2	2	1	14	9	3	0	1	8	1	1	0	0.00
Ferdie Schupp	2	2	1	10 1/3	11	2	2	2	9	1	0	0	1.74
Pol Perritt	3	0	0	8 1/3	9	2	2	3	3	0	0	0	2.16
Fred Anderson	1	0	0	2	5	4	4	0	3	0	1	0	18.00
Jeff Tesreau	1	0	0	1	0	0	0	1	1	0	0	0	0.00
Al Demaree	Did not play												
team total	6	6	3	51	54	21	17	11	28	2	4	0	3.00

REGULAR SEASON STATISTICS

	G	GS	CG	IP	H	ER	BB	SO	W	L	Pct	SV	ShO	ERA
Slim Sallee	34	24	18	216	199	52	34	54	18	7	.720	4	1	2.17
Rube Benton	35	25	14	215	190	65	41	70	15	9	625	3	3	2.72
Ferdie Schupp	36	32	25	272	202	59	70	147	21	7	.750	0	6	1.95
Pol Perritt	35	26	14	215	186	45	45	72	17	7	.708	1	5	1.88
Fred Anderson	38	18	8	162	122	26	34	69	8	8	.500	3	1	1.44
Jeff Tesreau	33	20	11	184	168	63	58	85	13	8	.619	2	1	3.08
Al Demaree (c)	15	11	1	78	70	23	17	23	4	5	.449	0	0	2.65
team total	158	158	92	1427	1221	360	327	551	98	56	.631	14	17	2.27

Total Attendance—186,654 Average Attendance—31,109 Winning Players's Share—$3,669 Losing Player's Share—$2,442

1917

Chicago White Sox vs. New York Giants

The New York Giants were, by 1917, "the best known team in baseball," according to *Baseball Magazine*. And, according to the records, the best team in all of baseball, period. No team had won more pennants, more games or had a higher winning percentage in the history of modern baseball than the Giants.

The Giants traced their proud ancestry back to 1880, when Jim "Smiling Jeems" Mutrie, a former player, and John B. Day, a businessman whose interests included tobacco and liquor, sat next to each other at a game between the Brooklyn Atlantics and the New York Mutuals. Finding that their interests in sponsoring a club were as mutual as the team on the field, they formed the Metropolitan Exhibition Company on the spot. Their first venture was the New York Mets, an independent team. In 1882 they joined the American Association and, hedging their bets, the following year took over the dead Troy (New York) Haymaker franchise and entered a team in the National League, forming the first baseball "syndicate." The National League team, which played its games at the old Polo Grounds at 110th Street and Fifth Avenue, became known as the Giants in 1888 when the stovepipe-hatted Mutrie, by then the manager of the team, remarked that his tall, broad-shouldered troops were "giants in action as well as stature."

Giants they became, a proud nickname for a proud team. Led by future Hall of Famers Tim Keefe and Mickey Welch on the mound and Buck Ewing and Roger Conner afield, they won two National League pennants in 1888 and 1889 and capped off both seasons by winning what was then the world's series (small "w," small "s"), defeating the second-place club in the league both years. However, the Brotherhood War, which broke out in 1890, turned the club from a prosperous venture into a losing proposition, and Day and Mutrie were all but wiped out.

By 1892 Day was done, finally losing control of the club to a syndicate of baseball knights who rescued the floundering franchise. Three years later they sold 51 percent to Andrew Freedman, a prominent Tammany politician. However, after seven lean years of what New York papers called "Freedmanism"—with the Giants finishing ninth, seventh, third, seventh, tenth, eighth and seventh—the remainder of the syndicate, most notably John T. Brush, owner of the Cincinnati ballclub, exerted their influence to prop up their investment; and to retaliate against the American League for raiding their ranks.

Brush went for the jugular, going after one of the American League's most famous names, and with him an entire franchise. The man was Baltimore manager John J. McGraw; the franchise was the Orioles. In a deal as complicated to understand three-quarters of a century later as it was then to consummate, Brush had McGraw ostensibly resign and sell his stock in the club back to the president of the club and sign a four-year contract with the Giants. His comrade-in-arms, longtime friend and teammate Wilbert Robinson, also supposedly sold his interest back to the president for the announced reason that he was using the proceeds to "secure enough money to buy out McGraw's interest in the saloon on North Howard Street, heretofore jointly owned by them." However, what Brush had done, acting as Freedman's covert agent, was to set up a scam whereby a lawyer selected by Brush would operate in Freedman's name, purchasing all of the club's stock for $50,000, thereby giving Freedman and New York first crack at the Baltimore players, with Brush and Cincinnati having second choice, and the other National League clubs to pay on a prorated basis for any athletes they wanted after the cream had been skimmed by New York and Cincinnati.

But no matter how complicated the maneuvering, one thing soon became certain: John McGraw needed help. For, as McGraw himself was later to relate, "When I took charge of the Giants the club was in last place by fourteen games—a good, safe margin. The attendance was almost nothing [and] when I first walked on the field to see my team I found Christy Mathewson playing first base."

But if McGraw needed help, he knew where to look for it—the American League in general and Baltimore in particular. He went to Freedman and pleaded his case: "With a club in last place by fourteen games in the middle of the season, there's little chance of us doing much this year. We've got to build for next season." Then he took out the list of 23 players assigned to him and crossed out nine names with one stroke of the pencil. "And you can begin by releasing these." Freedman was flabbergasted. "But you can't do that," he fuffumped. "Those players cost me a lot of money; they represent nearly $14,000." McGraw was unmoved. "The club wouldn't be any worse off without them. And their salaries for the rest of the season would amount to more than that. We would really be saving money," he concluded, now sure of his ground and more sure of Freedman's penurious position.

Freedman could only ask, "What will you do for others?" already sensing the answer. It was quickly forthcoming: "I'm going to get Kid Elberfeld, Fielder Jones, Ed Delehanty, George Davis . . ."

"Stop right there!" Freedman ordered. "I won't have George Davis on my club. He's been here and I don't like him. I wouldn't give him $3500 a year. I just won't have him . . . and that's final."

McGraw, however, would not be deterred. "I'm going to have him, Mr. Freedman. He's a great player and I need him. I *am* the manager, you know."

Freedman threw up his hands. And opened his purse. He knew, as all of baseball would know, that McGraw was indeed "*the* manager."

McGraw signed Elberfeld, Jones and Delehanty. However, a subsequent agreement between the two leagues prevented him from playing them. But if these three players were vagrant thoughts, McGraw's ambitious plan to stock the Giants with stars from other teams was not. Soon McGraw's handpicked team began to take shape. Here a George Davis and a Sam Mertes from the Chicago White Sox; there a Mike Donlin from the Reds, a George Browne from the Phillies and a Bill Dahlen from the Dodgers; and everywhere an ex-Oriole—Dan McGann, Roger Bresnahan, Billy Gilbert and Joe McGinnity.

But Freedman was a man of limited means—and even more limited imagination. And when McGraw brought him Davis's contract, it was the straw that broke Freedman's back. "I'll never forget the expression on Andrew Freedman's face when I came back from a raiding trip with George Davis's contract in my pocket," McGraw was to relate years later. "I tossed it on the table. It called for a salary of $6500. And this was the man Freedman said he wouldn't give $3500."

That was *it* for Freedman. He sold his interest in the Giants to Brush at the end of the season and retired from baseball, thus ending the Giant's most futile era and signaling the start of their most fertile one—the reign of John J. McGraw and John T. Brush.

With Brush's backing ("He was heart and soul with me in my plan to build up a club. He didn't care what players I bought or what I paid for them as long as my judgment dictated their purchase."), McGraw built a proud and mighty franchise. His all-new team finished second in 1903, first in 1904 and 1905, second in 1906, fourth in 1907, second in 1908 by one game (the year of the "Merkle Boner"), third in 1909, second in 1910 and first again in 1911 and 1912. When Brush died in the winter of 1912, his son-in-law, Harry Hempstead, took over control of the team and left McGraw to his own devices. And McGraw's devices were winning, winning and more winning. He again finished first in 1913, then second in 1914, eighth in 1915 (but only 3½ games out of the first division), fourth in 1916. And 1917 was to be another year for winning.

John McGraw was an inspiration to his team and a hate object to the rest of the league. But when all was said and done, McGraw inspired more players to greater heights than any other manager in the history of baseball. He was the reason why Larry Doyle, the young second baseman McGraw brought up in 1907, exulted, "Gee, it's great to be young and a Giant!"

McGraw, who had been the New York Giants since his arrival in New York in 1902, had continually been wooed by other clubs, even other leagues. But he had often expressed his feeling that "New York is the only place after all; I have done my best work there, and I want to stick with the Giants as long as I am in baseball." To insure that he did, Giants president Harry Hempstead signed McGraw to a new five-year contract on the eve of the 1917 campaign, which called for an annual salary of $40,000—"the largest salary ever paid to any man in baseball," announced Hempstead—and which also contained a bonus clause which said, "if the Giants have a good year Mr. McGraw will get more money than the president of the club."

One New York paper, the *World*, editorialized: "It would have been a baseball calamity if McGraw had left the Giants. New York fans always have regarded him as the man behind the gun. It is true that Christopher Mathewson deserved much of the credit when the Giants won pennants in 1904, 1905, 1911, 1912 and 1913, but it was McGraw's incomparable skill as a manager that surrounded Matty with winning players. Matty has gone but McGraw remains, ready and eager to repeat his former triumphs."

McGraw was still the same McGraw who had inspired so many players for so long and been given the nickname "The Little Napoleon" by his followers and "The Little Round Man" by his players. But his players, who had won five pennants in ten years, were not the same; many of them had grown long in the tooth and had long since departed. Gone were Mathewson, as well as pitchers Rube Marquard, Red Ames and Hooks Wiltse. Gone were catcher Chief Meyers, infielders Red Merkle, Larry Doyle, Art Delvin and Al Bridwell. Gone also were outfielders Red Murray, Fred Snodgrass and Josh Devore.

These men had now all been replaced, and like the ax which had had its head and handle replaced so many times that, while it no longer resembled its original state, it still was, to many baseball fans, the same unit—the New York Giants, with new faces and new names, doing battle at the same old stand under the same old manager, John J. McGraw.

The money invested by Hempstead in McGraw's contract was more than equalled by the amount he laid out to get McGraw the players he needed to build the Giants into a winner. More than $80,000 was spent to purchase the contracts of such Federal League standouts as outfielders Edd Roush and Benny Kauff, third baseman Bill McKechnie, catcher Bill Rariden and pitcher Fred Anderson. And another $10,000 was sent to the St. Louis Cardinals for the contract of pitcher Slim Sallee. McGraw then started using his well-stocked roster like trading cards, sending Roush and McKechnie to the Reds for Buck Herzog and picking up Heinie Zimmerman from the Cubs, Rube Benton from the Reds and pitcher Pol Perritt from the Cards. Blending these new additions with holdovers like George Burns, Davy Robertson, Jeff Tesreau and Art Fletcher, McGraw put together a team which he believed "was capable of winning the pennant this year [1917]."

But still, winning in 1917 would not be easy. For the National League, between 1914 and 1919, had a different team winning the pennant each year, the only time in baseball history this happened in six successive years. However, the one big accomplishment was that of John J. McGraw, whose Giants won more games in the National League those six years than any other club—a small measure of consistency in an era when little existed.

The team that McGraw had built differed mightily from his previous editions. The pitching staff—which only two years before had been ridiculed by writer Heywood Broun for the constant use of pitchers Ferdie Schupp and Rube Schauer as one where "It never Schauers, but it Schupps"—was now well balanced. With little Ferdie Schupp winning well-pitched game after well-pitched game, 21 in all, Slim Sallee putting together a personal winning streak of ten in a row—the longest streak in three years—on his way to 18 wins overall, and Rube Benton throwing in with nine straight wins and 15 in toto, the Giants' staff carried the club to the front. At bat they had two of the league's six .300 hitters in Kauff and Burns, the majors' co-leader in homers in Davy Robertson, and the leader in RBIs in Heinie Zimmerman. They were to lead the league in home runs, stolen bases, fielding, ERA and saves; they were to lead the league in the standings for all but two weeks of the season.

After the Giants had completed a western road trip in August that saw them win 12 of 17 games, they began to look like a good bet to win the pennant. Columnist Bugs Baer wrote, "The Giants have become in a fortnight a lively 4 to 1 betting proposition for pennant honors." It was more a gimmie than a gamble, as the Giants opened up a ten-game lead over the Phillies and waltzed home, clinching the title on September 24 as Slim Sallee beat the St. Louis Cards for McGraw's sixth National League pennant.

The Giants' opponent in the Series was the Chicago White Sox, who had won their first pennant since 1906, winning 100 games and finishing nine games in front of their nearest pursuer. The Giants and the White Sox had met before in post-season play, touring the world after the 1913 season. But this time it was different—it was a World Series, not a world tour.

The 1917 Series opened up in Chicago amid a backdrop of patriotic fervor, for America was at war. The stands at Comiskey Park were festooned with red, white and blue bunting, and the home team, the White Sox, wore uniforms bearing the same colors: the oversized "S" on their shirts was red and blue against a white background and their white stockings were banded with blue and red stripes.

Thousands of White Sox fans jammed into Comiskey Park to watch their beloved, and to razz the likes of "Muggsy" McGraw and Heinie Zimmerman—who had never been able to take it and was known to have a hot temper and "rabbit ears"—and take their first look at Benny Kauff, the legendary "Federal League Ty Cobb."

It was Eddie Cicotte and his unbeatable "shineball" against Slim Sallee. And although George Burns hit Cicotte's fifth pitch over second to start the game, it was only one of seven hits Cicotte gave up all day, as the White Sox won 2–1 in what *Spalding's Official Baseball Record* called "one of the best—if not the best—world series game that has been played since this series was inaugurated." The winning run came in the bottom half of the fourth when Hap Felsch hit a long drifting fly toward left center field. Both Burns and Kauff ran for the ball and just as Burns camped under it a capricious gust of wind carried the ball over his head and into the bleachers for a home run.

The second game, played on Sunday, October 7—the first Series game ever played on a Sunday—was preceded by a presentation of a $50 Liberty Bond to Hap Felsch, the hero of the day before, by entertainer Al Jolson, who had stolen away from his touring show, *Robinson Crusoe, Jr.*, to join the thousands at Comiskey Park. The White Sox manager called on his 16-game winner, Urban "Red" Faber, while McGraw started his ace, Ferdie Schupp, in an attempt to even up the Series.

However, Schupp was treated neither to Chicago's famed hospitality nor to any mercy as the White Sox drove him from the box in the second inning and went on to win 7–2, taking a 2–0 lead back to New York for game three.

Game three was more of the same, pre-game presentations and pageantry. The day was officially designated as "Liberty Loan Day," with banners throughout the Polo Grounds announcing the million-dollar loan drive and a marching band playing patriotic marches in order to, in the words of Giants president Harry Hempstead, "disgorge bank notes from the 40,000 fans at the game." A group from Hartford, Connecticut, presented Benny Kauff with an ivory-headed cane, another gave a watch to Hank Gowdy, the first player to enlist in the service, and a group from Cook County, Illinois, presented their own favorite, Heinie Zimmerman, with a box of raspberries, delivered from their seats in the stands behind first base.

Cicotte, the first-game winner, went against Rube Benton, and this time came out a loser, 2–0. Davy Robertson went to the wall in deep right field to rob Chick Gandil of at least a double to end the White Sox fourth, and then, as it always seems to happen, came up to open the very next inning. He boomed a triple into almost the identical spot, scoring one of the Giants' two runs moments later—all they needed to win.

The next day Schupp came back to pitch a shutout, beating Red Faber and the Sox 4–0 on two Benny Kauff homers—one of which was irretrievably lost in a Polo Grounds rosebush —sending the Series back to Chicago tied up, and the White Sox back without having scored a run in their last 22 innings.

Game five, back in Chicago, looked like a continuation as the Giants jumped to a quick 2–0 lead off Reb Russell. Russell failed to get the first three batters out and was quickly replaced by manager Rowland, who brought back Eddie Cicotte to retire the side. By the end of five, it was 4–1, New York. But in the seventh, New York started to come apart, with Robertson letting a ball fall in front of him for a double, Herzog dropping a relay throw and the Sox scoring three runs to tie the score. In the eighth, Zimmerman made a bad throw and the Sox got four more hits and three more runs to win 8–5. The winning pitcher, in relief, was Red Faber, who had held the Giants hitless in their last two at-bats to preserve the win.

The sixth game—and, as it turned out, the last—saw Faber going back to the mound against Rube Benton. This time the Sox won without any of their four runs being earned. The first run, and one of the most famous in World Series history, came in the fourth inning. Eddie Collins led off by grounding to Zimmerman, who made a wild throw to first, allowing Collins to take second. Joe Jackson then lifted an easy fly to Robertson in right field, who dropped the ball, Collins advancing to third. Benton, bearing down, got the next hitter, Felsch, to tap back to the mound. Benton fielded the ball cleanly and ran to the third base line, turning Collins back to third. He then threw the ball to Zimmerman, who was covering the bag. As Benton made his throw to third, Giants catcher Bill Rariden advanced up the line, leaving home plate unprotected, with no one backing him up. Collins, seeing that Zimmerman had the ball and the bag both, turned back toward the plate, and, finding it uncovered, took off. Zimmerman, finding no one to throw the ball to, took off after Collins, chasing the man (who had speed enough to steal 743 career bases) across the plate for the first run. The White Sox were to score two more runs in the fourth and another in the ninth, when Kauff dropped a fly ball, to win the game and the Series 4–2, with Faber getting his third win.

Despite Faber's three wins, Kauff's two homers and Chicago's one big moment in the sun, the moment that will always be remembered is the one when Heinie Zimmerman chased Collins across home plate. He was crucified by the fans and vilified in the press, the long-running goat of the Series. One reporter, Hughie Fullerton, paraphrased Kipling's Gunga Din, ending it with, "I'm a faster man than you are, Heinie Zim!" But Zimmerman always claimed nobody was covering the plate. "Who was I supposed to throw the ball to—Klem?" he asked. "I was afraid he would," Umpire Bill Klem said when he heard Zimmerman's comment.

But Clarence "Pants" Rowland, manager of the victorious White Sox and coach at third base, had this postscript to add: "I was racing alongside Collins all the way from the coaching box to the plate. I know Zimmerman could have made a play at the plate, because Rariden called for the ball. But Zimmerman shouted, 'Get out of the way. I'll get this monkey myself!'"

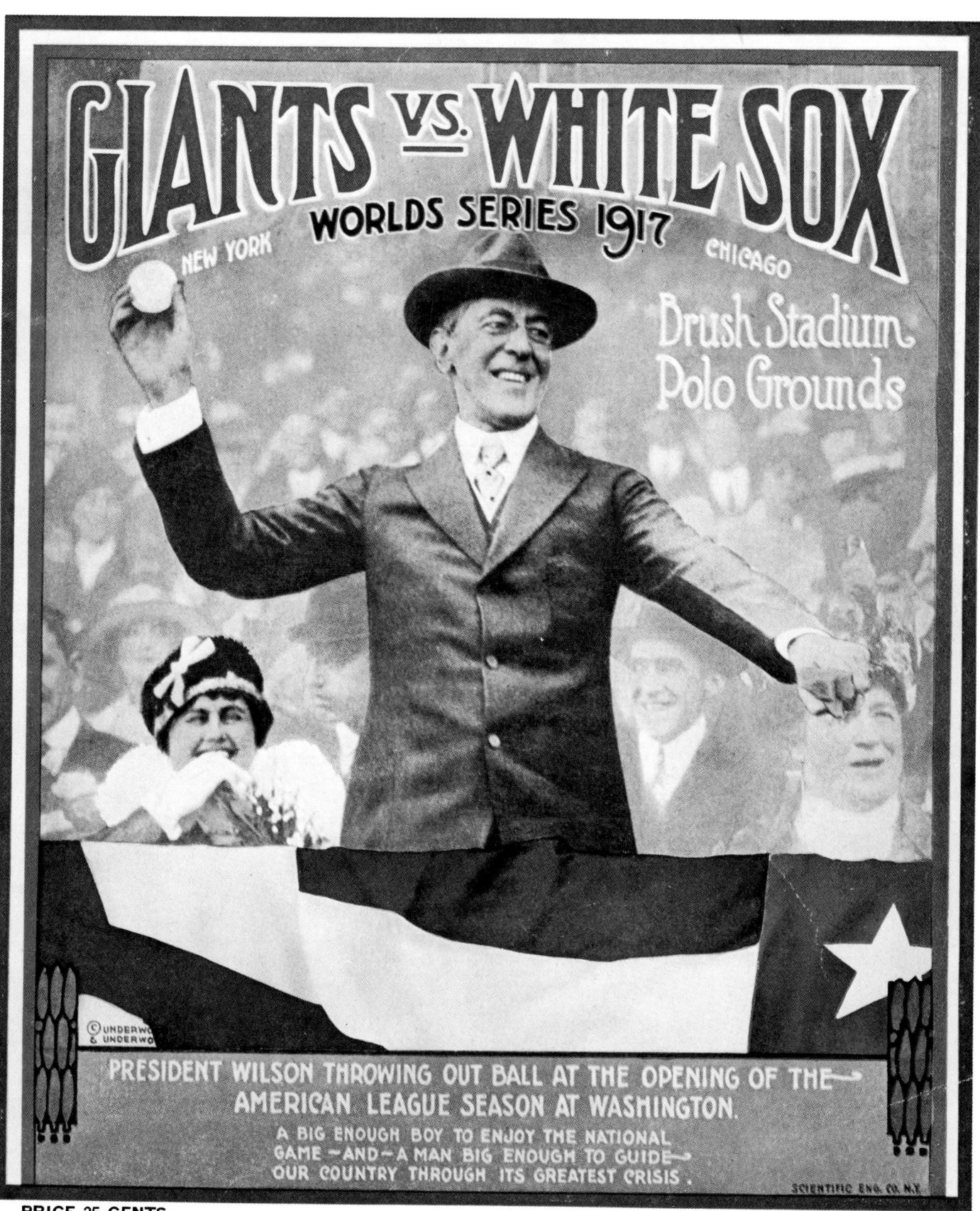

GIANTS vs. WHITE SOX

WORLDS SERIES 1917

NEW YORK   CHICAGO

Brush Stadium
Polo Grounds

PRESIDENT WILSON THROWING OUT BALL AT THE OPENING OF THE
AMERICAN LEAGUE SEASON AT WASHINGTON.

A BIG ENOUGH BOY TO ENJOY THE NATIONAL
GAME —AND— A MAN BIG ENOUGH TO GUIDE
OUR COUNTRY THROUGH ITS GREATEST CRISIS.

PRICE 25 CENTS   **HARRY M. STEVENS, Publisher**

MR. HARRY N. HEMPSTEAD
President, New York National League Baseball Club

MR. JOHN J. McGRAW
Manager of the New York Giants, 1903-1917.

MR. CHARLES A. COMISKEY
President of the Chicago American League Baseball Club
The Grand Old Roman of the National Pastime

ST. LOUIS BASE BALL CLUB ~ 1888
1 BOYLE   4 LYON   7 COMISKEY   10 KNOUFF
2 O'NEIL   5 McGARR   8 McCARTHY   11 LATHAM
3 MILLIGAN   6 KING   9 DEVLIN   12 HUDSON
                      13 ROBINSON

Number 7 in this group is Charles A. Comiskey as member of the St. Louis Baseball Club, the great St. Louis Browns who won the
A. A. League Championship in 1887 and 1888

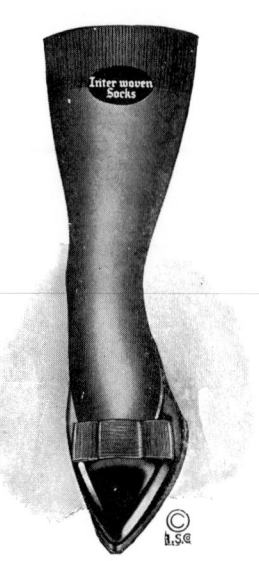

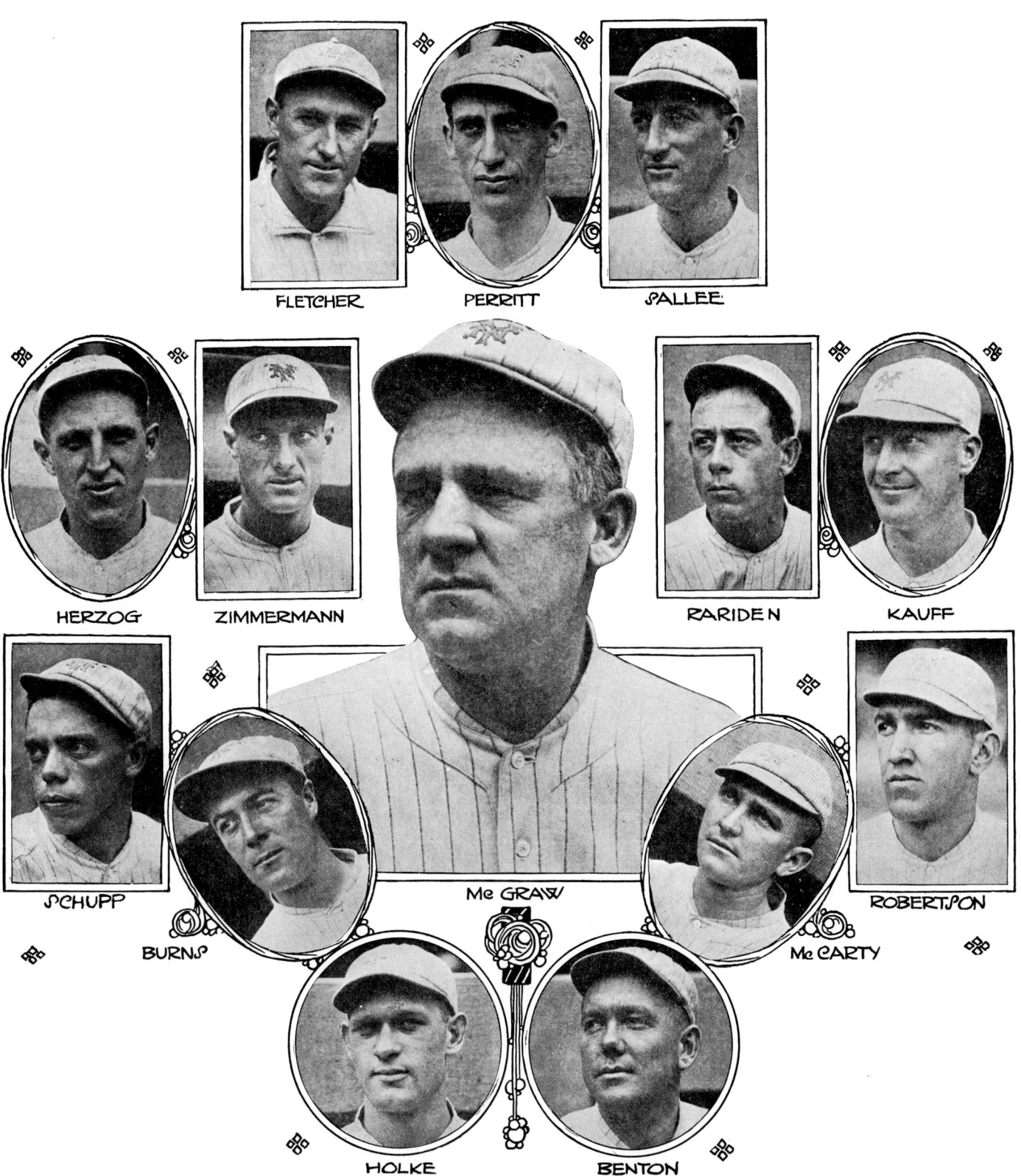

FLETCHER   PERRITT   SALLEE

HERZOG   ZIMMERMANN   RARIDEN   KAUFF

SCHUPP   BURNS   McGRAW   McCARTY   ROBERTSON

HOLKE   BENTON

Courtesy Evening Sun.

NEW YORK GIANTS AND THEIR LEADER

The
Corn Exchange Bank

William and Beaver Streets
NEW YORK CITY

*Member of the Federal Reserve System
and New York Clearing House*

Statement of the Condition of the Bank at the Close of Business Sept. 8th, 1917

Amount Due Depositors - - - - -	$131,621,632.49

To meet these deposits we have:

Cash in Vaults and Banks - - -	$27,831,535.97
Exchanges and Cash Items - - -	6,996,582.13
Demand Loans on Collateral - -	14,947,015.68
Bonds Owned - - - - -	28,685,780.00
Time Loans . - - . -	59,243,808.94
Bonds and Mortgages - - - -	813,116.25
Banking Houses and Lots - - -	3,681,320.00 142,199,158.97
Leaving Capital, Surplus and Undivided Profits of	$10,577,526.48

Thirty-eight branches located in New York City
Personal and business accounts respectfully solicited.

TRAVELERS' CHECKS.
CABLE TRANSFERS.

LETTERS OF CREDIT.
BILLS OF EXCHANGE.

WILLIAM A. NASH,
Chairman of the Board.

WALTER E. FREW,
President.

N. ASHLEY LLOYD
Treasurer, New York Baseball Club

CORNELIUS J. SULLIVAN
Vice-President, New York Baseball Club

NEW YORK PRESS REPRESENTATIVES

Back Row, Standing—A. M. Elias; A. R. Bendel (Newark News); Chas. Lovett (N. Y. Rep. St. Louis Globe-Dem.); Chas. A. Taylor (N. Y. Tribune); W. J. Slocum (Eve. Sun); Robt. Ripley (Globe); Sid Mercer (Globe); H. C. Hamilton (United Press); W. Dickinson (Telegraph); C. S. Brandebury (Associated Press); Jack Vicock (International News); Hyatt Daab (Eve. Telegram); George Underwood (N. Y. Sun).
Front Row, Seated—Bert Igoe (World); Harry J. Fink (North Side News); Harry Cross (Times); W. J. Macbeth (Tribune); Col. Jacob Ruppert (Pres. Yankees and Special Correspondent N. Y. Herald); Walter Trumbull (N. Y. World); Ed. B. Moss (Associated Press); William Hennigan (American); Fred Van Ness (N. Y. Journal).

The Electric Exposition and Motor Show of 1917

GRAND CENTRAL PALACE, Lexington Ave., 46th and 47th Sts.

OCTOBER 10th–20th

United States Government Exhibits

Army Signal Corps, Navy Recruiting, Submarine, Torpedo and Battle Cruiser Models, Light-house Service Equipment, Forestry Service Apparatus. Roads and Rural Engineering, Census Bureau and Weather Bureau.

Battle Bi-plane

(Loaned by Standard Aero Corp., Plainfield, N. J.)

New York State Exhibits

Models of Locks, Dams and Dam Operation.

War Bread Bakery

Model Dairy, Hat Manufacturing, Sugar Wrapping Machine, Electric Vehicles and Latest Electric Light, Heat and Power Devices.

Open from 11 a.m to 11 p.m.

ADMISSION
FIFTY CENTS

Red Cross

Work Rooms, Instructing Centre, Tea Room, Exhibit of Allies' Flags and Motion Pictures.

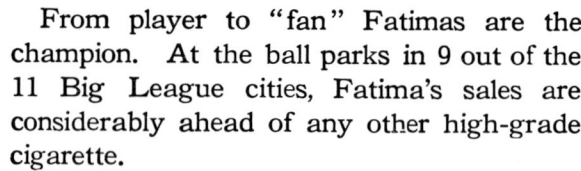

WHAT ABOUT THE WORLD SERIES IN THE TRENCHES?

Our American boys are fighting "OVER THERE" so you can be protected when you attend ball games OVER HERE.

They want smokes.   *Help us to send them.*

"OUR BOYS IN FRANCE TOBACCO FUND"

25 WEST 44th STREET   NEW YORK CITY.

16. Tesreau, Pitcher 18. Demaree, Pitcher 20. Onslow, Catcher 22. Lobert, Infield   24. Wilhoit, Outfield
17. Anderson, Pitcher 19. Gibson, Catcher 21. Smith, Infield 23. Baird, Infield 25. Murray, Outfield

NEW YORK

	1	2	3	4	5	6	7	8	9	10	AB	R	1B	SH	P.O	A	E
1. Burns — Left Field																	
2. Herzog — 2d Base																	
3. Kauff — Center Field																	
4. Zimmerman — 3d Base																	
5. Fletcher — Shortstop																	
6. Robertson / 7. Thorpe — R. Field																	
8. Holke — 1st Base																	
9. McCarty / 10. Rariden — Catcher																	
11. Schupp / 12. Sallee / 14. Perritt / 15. Benton — Pitcher																	

UMPIRES
31. Klem
32. Rigler

Earned Runs____ Two-Base Hits____ Three-Base Hits____ Home Runs____ Passed Balls____ Wild Pitches____
Bases on Balls____ Bases on Hit by Pitched Ball____ Struck Out____ Left on Bases____ Double Plays____ Time____

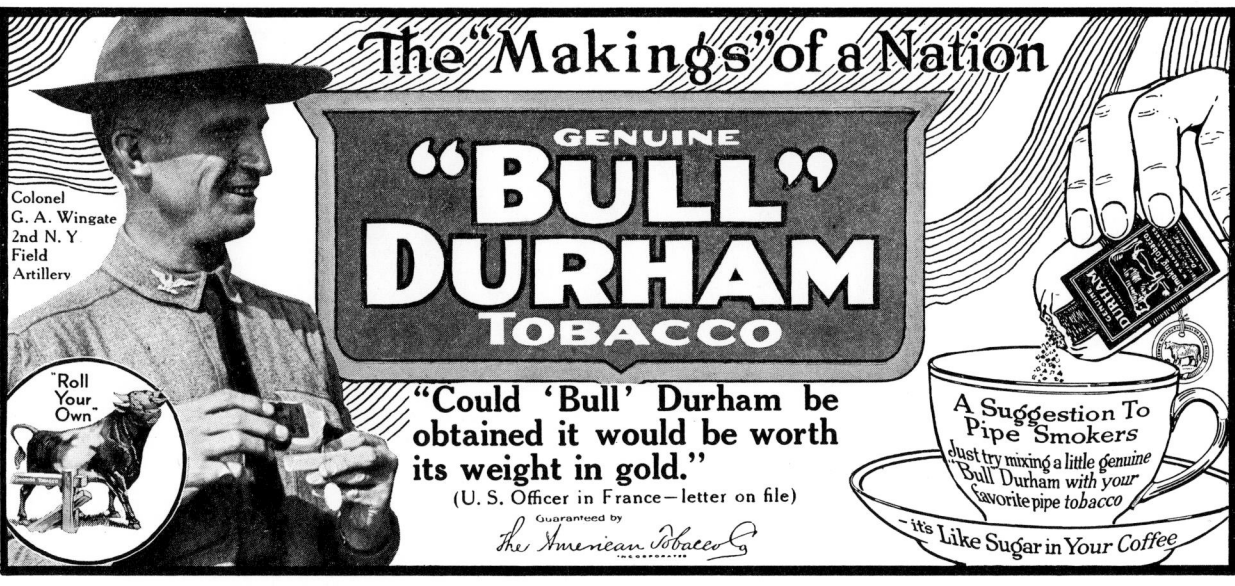

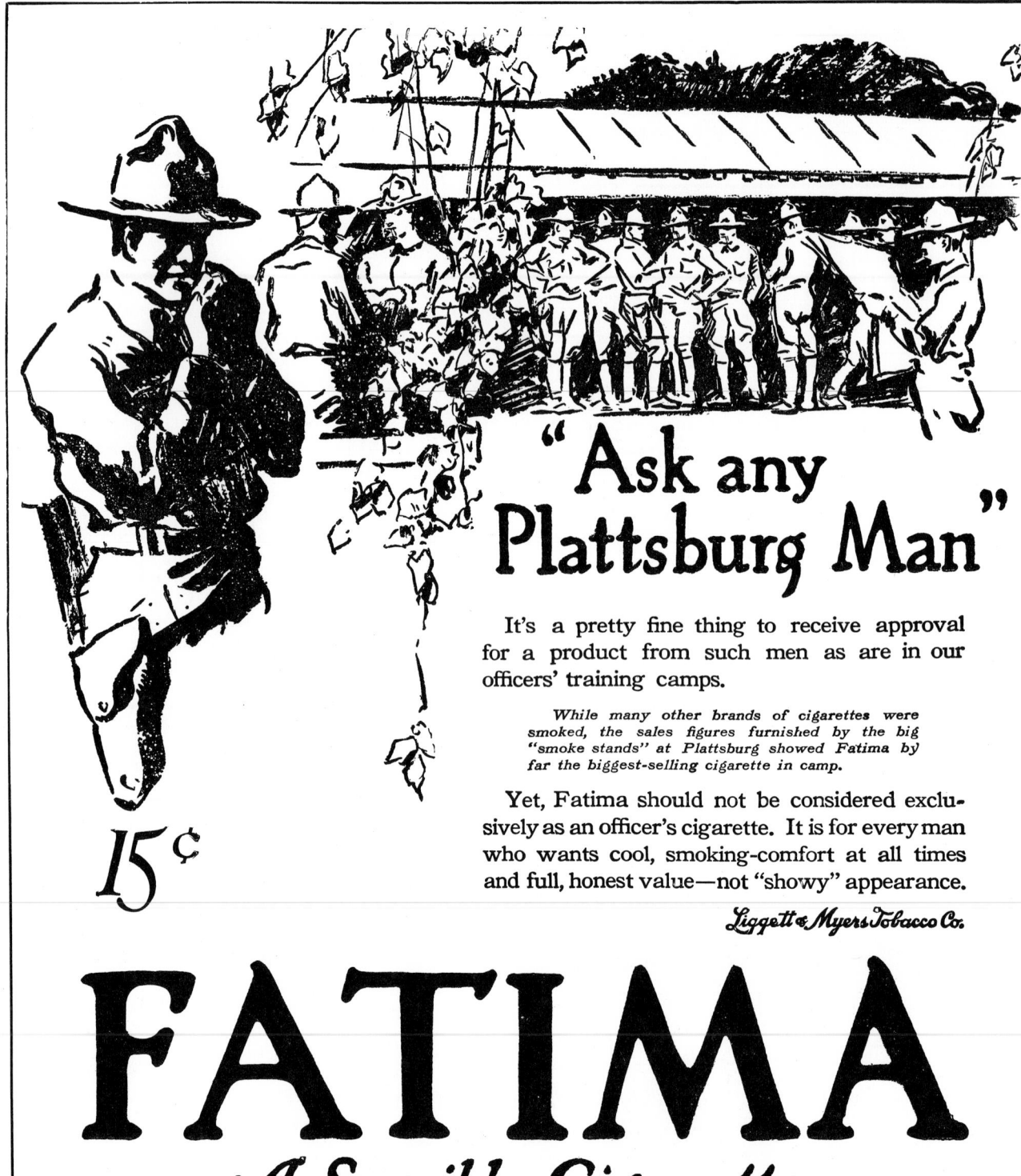
SOLD ON THE GROUNDS

17. Danforth, Pitcher	19. Wolfgang, Pitcher	21. Jenkins, Catcher	23. Hasbrook, Infield
18. Benz, Pitcher	20. Scott, Pitcher	22. Jourdan, Infield	24. Murphy, Outfield

CHICAGO

1. Leibold } Left Field
2. J. Collins }

3. McMullen   3d Base

4. E. Collins   2d Base

5. Jackson   Right Field

6. Felsch   Center Field

7. Gandil   1st Base

8. Weaver } Shortstop
9. Risberg }

10. Schalk } Catcher
11. Lynn }

12. Cicotte
14. Faber } Pitcher
15. Williams
16. Russell

UMPIRES
33. Evans
34. O'Loughlin

	1	2	3	4	5	6	7	8	9	10	AB	R	1B	SH	P.O	A	E

Earned Runs____Two-Base Hits____Three-Base Hits____Home Runs____Passed Balls____Wild Pitches___

Bases on Balls____Bases on Hit by Pitched Ball____Struck Out____Left on Bases____Double Plays____Time____

JOHN B. FOSTER, Secretary

J. J. MONHEIMER

HON. JOHN WHALEN

FRANK M. STEVENS

JAMES FOSTER, the man who built the Stadium

BOARD OF DIRECTORS, NEW YORK BASEBALL CLUB

MR. CLARENCE ROWLAND
Manager of the Chicago White Sox

Copyright Amer. Press Assn.

CHICAGO WHITE SOX
Pennant Winners of the American League, 1917
Left to Right, Top Row—Wolfgang, E. Collins, Cicotte, Benz, Hasbrook, Murphy, Weaver, Gleason, (Coach) Gandil, Lynn.
Middle Row—Schalk, Russell, J. Collins, Jourdan, Felsch, Manager Rowland, McMullen, Byrne, Danforth, Williams, Jenkins.
Front Row—Leibold, Jackson, and Riesberg.

DEAR OLD ARTHUR BELL
Superintendent for the Giants Ballyards
since 1880

CHICAGO PRESS REPRESENTATIVES
Travelling with the White Sox
Standing: James Crusinberry (Chicago
Tribune); Gus Axelsen (Chicago Herald);
Harry Niely (Chicago American). Seated:
Larry Woltz (Chicago Examiner); George
Robbins (Chicago News).

EDDIE BRANNICK
Asst. Secretary

CANDIES

sold exclusively on these grounds

Ask the Boys for

Milk Chocolate Almond Bars, 5c

Old Fashioned Molasses Candy, 10c

Washington Taffy, 5c

Pink Wrapper Sweet Chocolate, 5c

Lemon Sour Drops, 5c

Cream Peppermints, 10c

There are HUYLER'S Retail Stores in Chicago, Detroit, Toronto, Cleveland, Buffalo, Rochester, Syracuse, Albany, Boston, New Haven, New Rochelle, New York, Brooklyn, Newark, Atlantic City, Philadelphia, Baltimore, Norfolk, Richmond, Washington, Pittsburgh.

There are HUYLER'S dealers at practically every Army Training Camp.

Orders left with HUYLER'S Agents anywhere, or with HUYLER'S stores in any city, will be delivered free in any city where there is a HUYLER'S Store or HUYLER'S Agent.

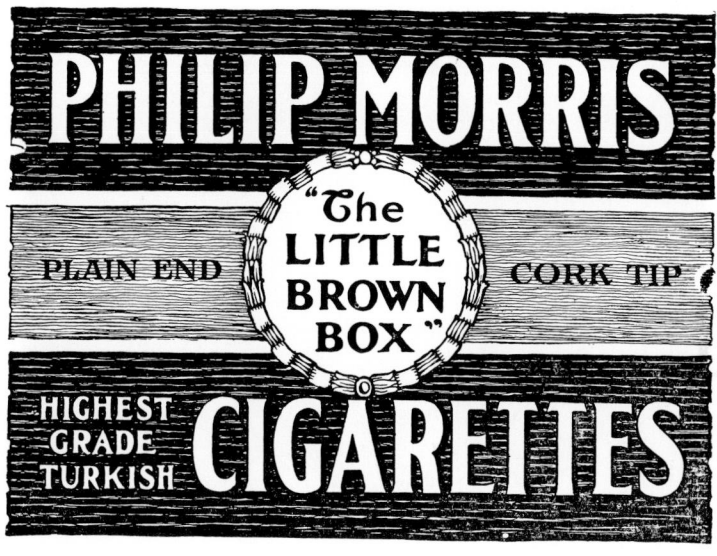

AUGUST HERMANN
PRES. NAT. COMM.

JOHN K. TENER
PRES. NAT. LEAGUE

B.B.JOHNSON
PRES. AMER. LEAGUE

JOHN HEYDLER
SECTRY. TO JOHN K. TENER

JOHN E. BRUCE
SECTRY. NAT. COMM.

WILLIAM HARRIDGE
SECTRY. TO B.B.JOHNSON

American Chicle Company

Adams Black Jack

Shouting reduces the voice
to a rasping whisper.
Get Adams Black Jack—

Bully for coughs and colds.
Then shout as loud as you please.
Sold on these Grounds.

*Adams Gum has been sold exclusively on the Polo Grounds for
22 consecutive years and up to now there has been no complaints*

M. B. Brown Printing & Binding Co.,
New York.

1919

Cincinnati Reds
vs.
Chicago White Sox

1919 WORLD SERIES COMPOSITE BOX

	Wins	Composite Line Score		Manager	Regular Season W L Pct. G. Ahead
Cincinnati Reds (N.L.)	5	5 1 2 10 3 9 2 2 1 0 – 35		Pat Moran	96 44 .686 9
Chicago White Sox (A.L.)	3	1 3 2 1 3 3 2 4 0 1 – 20		Kid Gleason	88 52 .629 3½

BATTING AND FIELDING

CINCINNATI REDS

	Pos	WORLD SERIES STATISTICS G AB R H 2B 3B HR RBI BB SO SB BA SA PO A E		Main Pos	REGULAR SEASON STATISTICS G AB R H 2B 3B HR RBI BB SO SB BA SA
Jake Daubert	1b	8 29 4 7 0 1 0 1 1 2 1 .241 .310 81 4 2		1b	140 537 79 148 10 12 2 44 35 23 11 .276 .350
Morrie Rath	2b	8 31 5 7 1 0 0 2 4 1 2 .226 .258 22 16 2		2b	138 537 77 142 13 1 1 29 64 24 17 .264 .298
Larry Kopf	ss	8 27 3 6 0 2 0 3 3 2 0 .222 .370 10 28 1		ss	135 503 51 136 18 5 0 58 28 27 18 .270 .326
Heinie Groh	3b	8 29 6 5 2 0 0 2 6 4 0 .172 .241 8 18 2		3b	122 448 79 139 17 11 5 63 56 26 21 .310 .431
Greasy Neale	rf	8 28 3 10 1 1 0 4 2 5 1 .357 .464 19 0 1		of	139 500 57 121 10 12 1 54 47 51 28 .242 .316
Edd Roush	cf	8 28 6 6 2 1 0 7 3 0 2 .214 .357 31 3 2		of	133 504 73 162 19 12 4 71 42 19 20 .321 .431
Pat Duncan	lf	8 26 3 7 2 0 0 8 2 2 0 .269 .346 9 0 0		of	31 90 9 22 3 3 2 17 8 7 2 .244 .411
Bill Rariden	c	5 19 0 4 0 0 0 2 0 0 1 .211 .211 25 3 1		c	74 218 16 47 6 3 1 24 17 19 4 .216 .284
Ivy Wingo	c	3 7 1 4 0 0 0 1 3 1 0 .571 .571 8 3 0		c	76 245 30 67 12 6 0 27 23 19 4 .273 .371
Sherry Magee	ph	2 2 0 1 0 0 0 0 0 0 0 .500 .500		of	56 163 11 35 6 1 0 21 26 19 4 .215 .264
Jimmy Smith	pr	1 0 0 0 0 0 0 0 0 0 0 — —		3b-ss-2b-of	28 40 9 11 3 1 3 10 4 8 1 .275 .525
Rube Bressler		Did not play		of-p	61 165 22 34 3 4 2 17 23 15 2 .206 .309
Hank Schreiber		Did not play		3b	19 58 5 13 4 0 0 4 0 12 0 .224 .293
Nick Allen		Did not play		c	15 25 7 8 0 1 0 5 2 6 0 .320 .400
Charlie See		Did not play		of	8 14 1 4 0 0 0 1 1 0 0 .286 .286
Hod Eller	p	2 7 2 2 1 0 0 0 0 2 0 .286 .429 0 2 0		p	38 93 10 26 3 3 1 13 0 16 2 .280 .409
Dutch Ruether	p-ph	3 6 2 4 1 2 0 4 1 0 0 .667 1.500 1 2 0		p	42 92 8 24 2 3 0 6 4 18 1 .261 .435
Jimmy Ring	p	2 5 0 0 0 0 0 0 0 2 0 .000 .000 1 3 0		p	32 62 3 6 1 0 0 1 1 20 0 .097 .113
Slim Sallee	p	2 4 0 0 0 0 0 0 0 0 0 .000 .000 1 4 0		p	29 74 5 14 2 2 0 7 6 20 1 .189 .270
Ray Fisher	p	2 2 0 1 0 0 0 0 0 1 0 .500 .500 0 6 1		p	26 59 11 16 1 0 0 5 4 7 1 .271 .288
Dolf Luque	p	2 1 0 0 0 0 0 0 0 1 0 .000 .000 1 0 0		p	31 32 3 4 1 1 0 2 3 1 0 .125 .219
Roy Mitchell		Did not play		p	7 10 0 0 0 0 0 0 0 0 0 .000 .000
Ed Gerner		Did not play		p	5 6 1 1 0 0 0 0 0 2 0 .167 .333
team total		8 251 35 64 10 7 0 34 25 22 7 .255 .351 216 92 12			140 4577 578 1204 135 83 20 489 405 368 143 .263 .342

Double Plays—7
Left on Bases—46

Manuel Cueto (of), Wally Rehg (of), Billy Zitzmann (of), Mike Regan (p) also played for the Reds during the season.

CHICAGO WHITE SOX

	Pos	WORLD SERIES STATISTICS G AB R H 2B 3B HR RBI BB SO SB BA SA PO A E		Main Pos	REGULAR SEASON STATISTICS G AB R H 2B 3B HR RBI BB SO SB BA SA
Chick Gandil	1b	8 30 1 7 0 1 0 5 1 3 1 .233 .300 79 2 1		1b	115 441 54 128 24 7 1 60 20 20 10 .290 .383
Eddie Collins	2b	8 31 2 7 1 0 0 1 1 2 1 .226 .258 21 31 2		2b	140 518 87 165 19 7 4 80 68 27 33 .319 .405
Swede Risberg	ss	8 25 3 2 0 1 0 0 5 3 1 .080 .160 23 30 4		ss-1b	119 414 48 106 19 6 2 38 35 38 19 .256 .345
Buck Weaver	3b	8 34 4 11 4 1 0 0 0 2 0 .324 .500 9 18 0		3b-ss	140 571 89 169 33 9 3 75 11 21 22 .296 .401
Nemo Leibold	rf-ph-cf	5 18 0 1 0 0 0 0 2 3 1 .056 .056 5 2 0		of	122 434 81 131 18 2 0 26 72 30 17 .302 .353
Happy Felsch	cf-rf	8 26 2 5 1 0 0 3 1 4 0 .192 .231 23 1 2		of	135 502 68 138 34 11 7 86 40 35 19 .275 .428
Joe Jackson	lf	8 32 5 12 3 0 1 6 1 2 0 .375 .563 16 1 0		of	139 516 79 181 31 14 7 96 60 10 9 .351 .506
Ray Schalk	c	8 23 1 7 0 0 0 2 4 2 1 .304 .304 29 15 1		c	131 394 57 111 9 3 0 34 51 25 11 .282 .320
Shano Collins	rf-cf	4 16 2 4 1 0 0 0 0 0 0 .250 .313 5 0 0		of	63 179 21 50 6 3 1 16 7 11 3 .279 .363
Fred McMullin	ph	2 2 0 1 0 0 0 0 0 0 0 .500 .500		3b	60 170 31 50 8 4 0 19 11 18 4 .294 .388
Eddie Murphy	ph	3 2 0 0 0 0 0 0 0 0 1 .000 .000		of	30 35 8 17 4 0 0 5 7 0 0 .486 .600
Byrd Lynn	c	1 1 0 0 0 0 0 0 0 0 0 .000 .000 1 0 0		c	29 66 4 15 4 0 0 4 4 9 0 .227 .288
Joe Jenkins		Did not play		c	16 19 0 3 1 0 0 1 1 1 1 .158 .211
Hervey McClellan		Did not play		3b-ss	7 12 2 4 0 0 1 1 1 1 0 .333 .333
Eddie Cicotte	p	3 8 0 0 0 0 0 0 0 3 0 .000 .000 0 6 2		p	38 86 5 14 0 1 0 8 9 18 0 .202 .222
Dickie Kerr	p	2 6 0 1 0 0 0 0 0 0 0 .167 .167 1 4 0		p	39 68 12 17 3 1 0 4 9 8 1 .250 .324
Lefty Williams	p	3 5 0 1 0 0 0 0 0 3 0 .200 .200 1 2 0		p	41 94 10 17 2 2 0 10 9 28 0 .181 .245
Roy Wilkinson	p	2 2 0 0 0 0 0 0 0 1 0 .000 .000 0 2 0		p	4 8 1 3 2 0 0 2 1 3 0 .375 .625
Bill James	p	1 2 0 0 0 0 0 0 0 1 0 .000 .000 0 0 0	a	p	5 14 2 2 0 0 0 2 0 2 0 .143 .143
Grover Lowdermilk	p	1 0 0 0 0 0 0 0 0 0 0 — — 0 1 0	b	p	20 34 1 3 0 0 0 1 0 19 1 .088 .088
Erskine Mayer	p	1 0 0 0 0 0 0 0 0 0 0 — — 0 0 0	c	p	6 7 0 0 0 0 0 0 0 3 0 .000 .000
Red Faber		Did not play		p	25 54 8 10 0 0 0 4 6 20 0 .185 .185
John Sullivan		Did not play		3b-ss	4 3 0 0 0 0 0 0 1 1 3 0 .000 .000
team total		8 263 20 59 10 3 1 17 15 30 5 .224 .297 213 115 12			140 4675 668 1343 218 70 25 571 427 358 150 .287 .380

Double Plays—9
Left on Bases—52

a—from St. Louis (A)
b—from Detroit and Boston (A)
c—from Pittsburgh (N)
Joe Benz (p), Dave Danforth (p), Tom McGuire (p), Win Noyes (p), Pat Ragan (p), Charlie Robertson (p), Reb Russell (p), Frank Shellenback (p) also played for the White Sox during the season.

PITCHING

CINCINNATI REDS

	WORLD SERIES STATISTICS G GS CG IP H R ER BB SO W L SV ERA		REGULAR SEASON STATISTICS G GS CG IP H ER BB SO W L Pct. SV ShO ERA
Hod Eller	2 2 2 18 13 5 4 2 15 2 0 0 2.00		38 30 16 248 216 66 50 137 20 9 .690 2 7 2.40
Dutch Ruetler	2 2 1 14 12 5 4 4 1 1 0 0 2.57		33 29 22 243 195 49 83 78 19 6 .760 0 3 1.81
Jimmy Ring	2 1 1 14 7 1 1 6 4 1 1 0 0.64		32 18 12 183 150 46 51 61 10 9 .526 3 2 2.26
Slim Sallee	2 2 1 13⅓ 19 6 2 1 2 1 1 0 1.35		29 28 22 228 221 52 20 24 21 7 .750 0 4 2.05
Ray Fisher	2 1 0 7⅔ 7 3 2 2 2 0 1 0 2.35		26 20 12 174 141 42 38 41 14 5 .737 1 5 2.17
Dolf Luque	2 0 0 5 1 0 0 0 6 0 0 0 0.00		30 9 6 106 89 31 36 40 9 3 .750 3 2 2.63
Rube Bressler	Did not play		13 4 1 42 37 16 8 13 2 4 .333 0 0 3.43
Roy Mitchell	Did not play		7 4 2 31 32 8 9 10 0 1 .000 0 0 2.32
Ed Gerner	Did not play		5 1 0 17 22 6 3 2 1 0 1.000 0 0 3.18
team total	8 8 5 72 59 20 13 15 30 5 3 0 1.62		140 140 89 1274 1104 316 298 407 96 44 .686 9 23 2.23

CHICAGO WHITE SOX

	WORLD SERIES STATISTICS G GS CG IP H R ER BB SO W L SV ERA		REGULAR SEASON STATISTICS G GS CG IP H ER BB SO W L Pct. SV ShO ERA
Eddie Cicotte	3 3 2 21⅓ 19 9 7 5 7 1 2 0 2.91		40 35 29 307 256 62 49 110 29 7 .806 1 5 1.82
Dickie Kerr	2 2 2 19 14 4 3 3 6 2 0 0 1.42		39 17 10 212 208 68 64 79 13 8 .619 0 1 2.89
Lefty Williams	3 3 1 16⅓ 12 12 12 8 4 0 3 0 6.61		41 40 27 297 265 87 58 125 23 11 .676 0 5 2.64
Roy Wilkinson	2 0 0 7⅓ 9 4 1 4 3 0 0 0 1.23		4 1 1 22 21 5 10 5 1 1 .500 0 1 2.05
Bill James	1 0 0 4⅔ 8 4 3 2 0 0 0 0 5.79	a	5 5 3 39 39 11 14 11 3 1 .750 0 2 2.54
Grover Lowdermilk	1 0 0 1 2 1 1 1 0 0 0 0 9.00	b	20 11 5 97 95 30 43 43 5 5 .500 0 0 2.78
Erskine Mayer	1 0 0 1 0 1 0 1 0 0 0 0 0.00	c	22 11 9 97 95 30 43 43 5 5 .500 0 0 2.78
Red Faber	Did not play		25 20 9 162 185 69 45 45 11 9 .629 2 0 3.83
John Sullivan	Did not play		4 2 1 15 24 7 8 4 0 1 .000 0 0 4.20
team total	8 8 5 71 64 35 27 25 22 3 5 0 3.42		140 140 87 1266 1245 427 342 468 88 52 .629 2 14 3.04

Total Attendance—236,928   Average Attendance—29,616   Winning Player's Share—$5,207   Losing Player's Share—$3,254

1919

Cincinnati Reds vs. Chicago White Sox

With the end of World War I, Johnny came marching home. But the world he came marching home to was entirely different from the one he had left. Morals were down and skirts were up. And on January 16, 1919, the Prohibition amendment to the Constitution was ratified. Morals would suffer even more.

Disenchanted Americans, believing that their privations and principles had failed to give them the promised peace they had fought for, turned from the rigors of problem solving to the rituals of pleasure seeking. From a gigantic laundry list of available diversions, they almost universally settled on one form of escapism—sports. And among the sports they embraced most avidly in their freewheeling mood was the sport of baseball. But by the end of 1919 America's love affair with baseball was to turn sour, another casualty in what was to become a losing battle against postwar immorality.

Much had happened to change the face of baseball during the four years of World War I: attendance, once proud testimony to baseball's growth, had fallen from over 6.3 million in 1913—the last prewar year—to 3 million by 1918. A new league, the Federal League, had declared war on the entrenched American and National Leagues, invading its sacred turf and raiding its ranks for players, with such established stars as Joe Tinker, "Three-Finger" Brown, George Mullen, Danny Murphy and Hal Chase succumbing to its big money offers. Others, like Ty Cobb, Tris Speaker and Walter Johnson, entertained offers, but stayed with their teams when the entire league anted up equivalent salaries. Several marginal franchises, seeking more secure ownership, had changed hands, including the Boston Braves, the Boston Red Sox, the Chicago Cubs, the St. Louis Browns and the St. Louis Cardinals. And, in the face of Secretary of War Newton Baker's edict to major league players to "work or fight," several major league stars, including Joe Jackson, Lefty Williams, Hap Felsch and Jeff Tesreau, had laid down their gloves to pick up wrenches at steel plants, while others, like Grover Cleveland Alexander, Christy Mathewson and Hank Gowdy, had enlisted. There were serious doubts as to whether baseball would even survive the war and, if it did, whether it would ever again rise to its exalted level of "National Pastime."

By 1919 the storm clouds looked like they were lifting, and baseball—together with everything else—began to head back to what Warren Harding would call normalcy. On January 10, the president of the New York Giants, Harry Hempstead, delivered a ringing speech in support of the game's future: "I truly believe the old game will thrive this year as it has not since the World War began in 1914." Then, four days later, believing his own campaign oratory, Hempstead took advan-

tage of the optimism he had showered on baseball by unloading the controlling interest in the team to a syndicate composed of Charles Stoneham, John J. McGraw and Francis X. McQuade for $1.3 million, personally thriving to the tune of over a million dollars. It came as no surprise to the establishment that Stoneham, whose occupation was officially listed as "curb broker," was, in reality, a racetrack owner and gambler. Such were baseball's strange bedfellows in 1919.

Ever since the formation of the National League the Giants and the Cincinnati Reds had formed a tandem that had continuously shuttled players—and even owners—back and forth between the two teams. Cincinnati owner John T. Brush had once traded his franchise for the entire New York team. He had then traded his aging pitcher, Amos Rusie, to the Reds for a young pitcher named Christy Mathewson. Others who had been given one-way—and in some instances round-trip—tickets between New York and Cincinnati included Jim Thorpe, Edd Roush, Heinie Groh, Fred Toney, Rube Benton, Buck Herzog, Bill McKechnie, Red Ames, Josh Devore, Eddie Grant, Bob Bescher, Art Fromme, Cy Seymour and "Turkey Mike" Donlin.

Now the New York–Cincinnati shuttle would go into operation again, for the team that Hempstead sold Stoneham included two men who would have a hand in making the Reds the National League champions in 1919. The first was Patrick J. Moran, former manager of the Philadelphia Phillies, who, in four years at the helm of the perennial tail-enders, had won 323 games and lost only 257—finishing first once, second twice and sixth in his last year, 1918, a season shortened by the war. Released by the Phillies at the end of 1918, Moran had signed on with the Giants as coach in early January. On January 30, the New York Giants gave the Reds permission to sign Moran as their field manager, taking the place of Christy Mathewson and Heinie Groh, two former Giants, who had brought Cincinnati home in third place in 1918. Moran, who had always been close to McGraw—as, indeed, every member of the Reds seemed to have been—immediately approached the "Little Napoleon" for a pitcher to take the place of Fred Toney, who had been traded to the Giants at the end of 1918. McGraw accommodated his old friend by trading him the tall left-hander, Slim Sallee, who had only an 8–8 record in 1918. Moran was to win the pennant and Sallee was to win 21 games for Moran, before going back to New York in 1920, after just a one-year-plus lend-lease.

There was yet another player whose name appeared on both rosters: Hal Chase. Chase was a brilliant left-handed first baseman, with few peers as a fielder, who, it was suggested by many, also thought left-handed. His "corkscrew mind" was used, several observers hinted, to perfect the fine art of throwing baseball games for fun and profit. Chase had played in the American League for nine years—gaining a reputation as the finest-fielding first baseman in baseball—before jumping to the new Federal League in 1914. It was there he earned a second reputation, one for skulduggery. When the Federal League disbanded after two financially disastrous seasons, no American League team would touch him. But Garry Herrmann, president of the Reds, bought his contract for the 1916 season. Chase rewarded Herrmann immediately by winning the National League batting championship in 1916. Even then, there was talk that Cincinnati manager Christy Mathewson suspected Chase's loyalty.

Those rumors came to a head late in 1918, when, just before he enlisted and went overseas, Mathewson formally charged Chase with throwing games. National League president Heydler conducted a full-scale investigation, but he was handicapped by Mathewson's absence and the fact that Matty had been advised by counsel that if he were to give an unsubstantiated deposition in support of his claim, he would face possible charges of libel.

Even while the investigation was going on, Giant manager John McGraw announced that if Chase was vindicated, he had a job open for him at first base. Heydler's position was, at best, compromised. "Here I am trying to prove the charges that Mathewson, McGraw's close friend, has made against this man," he complained to an associate, "and McGraw already is offering him a job." Despite the fact that Heydler thought Chase guilty, he had "no proof that will stand up in a court of law," and on February 6, 1919, exonerated him of "any wrongdoing." Thirteen days later McGraw sent catcher Bill Rariden and first baseman Walter Holke to the Reds for Chase's contract, and Chase withdrew his claims against Cincinnati and signed with the Giants. In New York, ironically, he was to be joined by Mathewson, who returned from Europe to become a coach for McGraw. It was something that would come back to haunt baseball after the strange and sordid story of the 1919 World Series finally came to light.

The pennant race began on April 23 with what the newspapers called "the largest attendance" in major league history. Moran took his troops immediately to the front, where they momentarily faltered and—despite a no-hitter by shineball artist Hod Eller, and a dramatic victory over Brooklyn in which they scored ten runs in the thirteenth inning to win 10-0—Cincinnati fell to second, behind the Giants. But even then, Moran and his team became the darling not only of the Ohio Valley, but of the National League and the nation as well. The former Phillies manager was given a "Day" by his former fans in Philadelphia on May 26. By July 6, two days after the magic day when the pennant winner is supposedly decided, the Reds went back into first place.

With Edd Roush leading the National League in batting and the Reds' pitching staff—comprised of Slim Sallee, Hod Eller, Dutch Ruether, Ray Fisher, Jimmy Ring and Dolf Luque—leading the league in shutouts, fewest hits given up and ERA, the Reds perfected their hold on first by August 2 and began to pull away from the field.

The entire Ohio Valley, which had not had a winner in a half-century—since the great Reds team of 1869—went almost as wild with its Reds as Attorney General A. Mitchell Palmer did with his, sending all suspected "reds" back "home" to Russia, "where they belonged." The mania in Ohio became so intense that all attendance records at Redland Field were

broken and the National Commission of Baseball extended the number of games in the World Series to best five out of nine for the purported reason that baseball enthusiasts throughout the nation "could see all they wished" of the Series. However, the *Spalding Official Baseball Record* of 1920 also advanced the theory that the series was extended because "the Ohio Valley never had a previous event of the kind" and Garry Herrman, president of the Reds, was, incidentally, head of the National Commission.

The Reds solidified their lead in August by winning four double-headers in ten days, and clinched their first-ever pennant on September 16. They finished the season with 96 wins and a nine-game lead over second-place New ed their first-ever pennant on September 16. They finished the season with 96 wins and a nine-game lead over second-place New York.

Meanwhile, over in the American League, the Chicago White Sox, bolstered by the return of Joe Jackson, Hap Felsch and Lefty Williams from their wartime service in the factories, won their second pennant in three years. The Sox, ahead of the pack almost all of the season, built up a 7½ game lead over the Cleveland Indians and finally staggered across the finish line 3½ games in front, winners of but 88 games, the lowest number of wins of any Series entrant in history—with the notable exception of the two teams in the 1918 Series, the result of a shortened season.

Nevertheless, the Sox were immediately installed as a 7–5 favorite. The fact that the American League had won eight of the last nine Series coupled with the fact that many, including Ed Barrow, were calling the White Sox "one of the greatest teams of all time," added to their aura of invincibility.

Two factors had been overlooked by the so-called experts. One was the inherent weakness of the White Sox' pitching staff—a pitching staff of two, Eddie Cicotte and Claude "Lefty" Williams, who had accounted for 60 percent of the team's wins, the most any two pitchers had ever won for any Series team. Whereas the Reds' pitching staff had compiled a 2.23 ERA and thrown 23 shutouts, the Sox' staff had a 3.04 ERA and but 14 shutouts, the second highest ERA of any World Series staff and the fewest shutouts by any staff. To further attest to the thinness, even raggedness, of Chicago's staff, 17 pitchers had taken their place on the mound for the Sox in 1919, the most of any pennant winner until then.

But there was one other factor the experts had not taken into consideration: the cupidity of the White Sox players, and the moral climate that made that cupidity bloom. Almost from the day the season ended on September 29, rumors began flying of a "fix," but most dismissed them as exactly that, rumors. It seemed financially impossible, for the teams would be playing for the largest World Series pot in history. And even if financially possible, it seemed physically improbable: how could any one man affect the outcome of the games that much?

And yet, the rumors increased in crescendo, with substance being lent to the rumors by the shifting of the odds in Cincinnati's favor and by the invasion of Cincinnati by what was then politely known as "the sporting crowd."

The scene in Cincinnati the week of October 1 was pure carnival. Devotees, dilettantes and denizens of the netherworld all descended upon the city from points east, west and south, ready for almost anything. Any "action." And there was plenty to be found. All the high rollers were in town. Sport Sullivan, betting commissioner for the likes of George M.

Cohan, was there. So were former featherweight champion Abe Attell, Nicky Arnstein and "Sleepy" Bill Burns, former big league pitcher—all emissaries of Arnold Rothstein. And so was Hal Chase, recently released by the Giants under a cloud. All came with money that seemed to be crying out "Bet me! Bet me!" And bet they did, as the odds changed from 7–5, Chicago, to 6–5, Cincinnati. Something was going on. Later testimony would reveal exactly what "something" was: the Series had been fixed.

Baseball had had its scandals before. In 1877, four members of the Louisville Grays were expelled from baseball for "hippodroming" (the then-fashionable word for throwing games), not only threatening the existence of the embryonic national game, but also forcing two teams out of the National League. Throughout the years other such scandals had been hinted at, but none had ever surfaced. Now, there was more than a hint in the air; there were rumors, tantalizing in their intensity, and persistent enough to be accepted as fact—the "fix was in."

But if the "fix was in," who was in on the fix? Many members of both teams were named. The most recurrent rumors named members of the Reds because of Hal Chase's former presence on the team and his accessibility to them, even now.

Cincinnati superstar Edd Roush recalls Reds manager Pat Moran calling over pitcher Hod Eller before the fifth game and asking him, "Hod, I've been hearing rumors about sellouts. Not about you, not about anybody in particular, just rumors. I want to ask you a straight question and I want a straight answer: Has anybody offered you anything to throw a game?" Eller, in his Indiana drawl, answered "Yup!" as the clubhouse fell into a hush. "After breakfast this morning, a guy got on the elevator with me, and got off at the same floor I did," he continued. "He showed me five thousand-dollar bills and said they were mine if I'd lose the game today." Moran could only ask, "And what did you say?" "I said that if he didn't get damn far away from me real quick he wouldn't know what hit him. And the same went if I ever saw him again." Moran, accepting his reply as gospel, handed him the ball and said, "OK, you're pitching today. But one wrong move and you're out of the game."

Another Cincinnati starter, Dutch Ruether, had also been approached, having gone out for drinks with known gamblers the night before game one, when, it was rumored, he had lifted up one too many cups of kindness for auld lang syne. Years later, Ruether, like Eller, would attempt to get at one of his tormentors. Bill Veeck remembers Ruether meeting, for the first time since 1919, a gambler named "Nig" who had offered him a bribe before game one, and Ruether chasing him around the room with malice in his heart and a cue stick in his hand.

Who had gotten to whom? The answer was provided to those in the know on the second pitch of the first inning by Chicago White Sox pitcher Eddie Cicotte. Cicotte, one of baseball's great shineball pitchers—he carried transparent paraffin on his trousers and used it to make the ball slide off his fingers and break just as it reached the plate, something like a spitter—also had great control, hitting just two batters during the season and walking just 49 in 306 innings. But, on the second pitch to Morrie Rath, the Reds' lead-off batter, he hit him in the back, signaling that the fix was on.

Cicotte's "signal" was to become the first run of the Series.

But Cicotte's real contribution was to come in the fourth inning when Cincinnati scored five runs. Cicotte, who later admitted he had thrown the game by "giving Cincinnati easy balls and putting them right over the plate. A baby could have hit them . . .," gave up, in succession, a single to Greasy Neale, a single to Ivy Wingo, a triple to opposing pitcher Dutch Ruether, a double to Morrie Rath and a single to Jake Daubert. In all, five runs and the game.

Cicotte's form reversal impressed many observers; the odds jumped to 8–5 on the Reds and doubts in the minds of some became reality in the minds of others. Hughie Fullerton, the perspicacious columnist for the Chicago Herald and Examiner, was forced to admit, "I don't like what I saw out there today. There is something smelly. Cicotte doesn't usually pitch like that."

The "smell" continued in game two as White Sox pitcher Lefty Williams took up where Cicotte had left off, "throwing" his game in as improbable a manner as Cicotte had thrown his. Williams, noted for his control—having given up only 58 bases on balls in 1919 in 297 innings pitched—picked the same inning, the fourth, to turn artificiality into burlesque, giving up a walk to lead-off man Rath, another to Cincinnati third baseman Heinie Groh and still another to catcher Pat Duncan. Sandwiching in a single and triple for three runs, he lost a four-hitter, 4–2.

After the second game disbelief grew to doubt, which, in turn, blossomed into suspicion. A reporter sought out John McGraw and asked him if he had seen anything. McGraw could only answer, "What do you mean, anything?" Ray Schalk, the Chicago catcher, had also seen something; he had seen his signals waved off for two straight games. After the second game he accosted Lefty Williams outside the locker room, and, according to Joe Villa of the New York Sun, sailed into him with flying fists in an attempt to vent his frustrations.

There was one other man who also had seen something—Charles Comiskey, the president of the Chicago White Sox. Known as "The Old Roman," Comiskey was almost as enduring and imperishable as baseball itself, having been associated with the national game since he joined the old St. Louis Browns in 1882. Renowned as a leader, he was selected by his old friend, Ban Johnson, to head up the St. Paul franchise in the Western League in preparation for the invasion of Johnson's new major league into Chicago in 1901. Over the course of 19 years Comiskey had seen his team win the very first American League pennant in 1901, his "Hitless Wonders" win the 1906 Series and repeat in 1917 as World Champions. During their 19 years of existence, his White Sox had compiled one of the most successful records in the league, averaging 81 wins a year and becoming one of baseball's most profitable premier franchises.

The White Sox, however, bore more than the Comiskey stamp of identification; they also resembled his personality—tough, resourceful and proud. But even more than that, they were driven, like Comiskey, by a need, even a love, for money. For Comiskey, like so many self-made men of that era, was not one to indulge in financial overkill. Instead, like the paternalistic Pullmans and others whom he had known all his life, he was given to rewarding those he favored with something other than money—other perks, like job security. He had given many of his hand-picked favorites within his fiefdom jobs within the organization: Nixey Callahan, a journeyman player who had been with his first White Sox team as a pitcher, infielder and outfielder, became his manager for five years; Kid Gleason, the old infielder who had been his coach for many years, was made manager of the 1919 team after Comiskey had fired "Pants" Rowland for finishing sixth in the war-shortened 1918 season. But his players fared less fortunately, with only second baseman Eddie Collins getting anything like a star's wages. The others were paid what Comiskey could get away with paying them.

Not only did Collins's salary act as a decisive force in separating the Sox into two camps—the "Lily-Whites" and the anti-Collins faction, soon to become known as "The Black Sox"—but it also acted as the catalyst for several of the members of the team transferring their allegiance from Comiskey to coin.

The ringleader in effecting this transference was Chick Gandil, the team's first baseman. Gandil, called by Cicotte "the master of ceremonies" in arranging the fix, had enlisted the aid of utility infielder Fred McMullin and shortstop Swede Risberg in putting together his cabal of fixers. He then approached such netherworld figures as Chase, who, together with Abe Attell and Nicky Arnstein, close associates of noted gambler Arnold Rothstein, underwrote the fix, taking advantage of the fact, as Westbrook Pegler was to write 20 years later, that they knew the Sox were underpaid.

When the larcenous liaison was made, Gandil started rounding up some of those in his clique to throw in with him. Corruption crept in from every available avenue. He called Lefty Williams to one side in front of the Hotel Ansonia in New York the day after his demands were met by the gamblers and, according to Williams, "put this thing to me." Cicotte confessed later that he yielded to the collective pressures of Gandil, Risberg and McMullin, and he, too, became a part of the unholy alliance, using the money to pay off the mortgage on his farm. Jackson, scared of Risberg—"Swede is a hard guy"—was pressured into the conspiracy by Gandil and Risberg. Felsch was brought in by Gandil. Weaver became an interested party, brought into meetings by the rest of the group, but never a participant in the actual throwing of games. Together, these eight men were to go down in infamy as "The Black Sox," and together they were to write the sorriest chapter in the history of baseball.

But for the moment, their cupidity was not known. All that was known was that something was wrong. Very wrong. The Sox, on paper the stronger of the two teams, were down two games to none and rumor had it that both games had been thrown. Those rumors reached the ears of Comiskey himself. But Comiskey could not turn to American League president Johnson because of an internecine feud he was presently having with him. Having shut himself off from the president of his own league, Comiskey could only turn to the two other members of the National Commission, National League president John Heydler and Cincinnati Reds' president Garry Herrmann. Unable to sleep after Williams's inexplicable loss in the second game, Comiskey participated in a scene reminiscent of a Marx Brothers movie, sneaking down the corridors into Heydler's room at the Hotel Stinton. Heydler heard out "The Old Roman," but believed his suspicions were nothing more than those of a man whose team had lost two in a row to an underdog. Nevertheless, he agreed to serve as an emissary, and, donning his dressing gown, he tiptoed up the same corridor to Johnson's room to convey Comiskey's suspicions. But Johnson was unmoved by anything Comiskey had to say, especially now, and responded, at the top of his lungs, somewhat sleepily and somewhat drunkenly, "That's the yelp of a beaten cur!"

The next day, though, it was not a "beaten cur," but an unbeatable Kerr that was the story. Those "in the know" figured that the gamblers who had engineered the fix had won about $500,000 on the first two games in the Series and thought so little of little Dickie Kerr, a diminutive rookie southpaw who had won just 13 games, that they attempted to pyramid their winnings in the third game. Kerr, unlike Cicotte and Williams, pitched masterfully, and allowed just three hits as the White Sox won their first game, 3–0. Stories began to grow on stories: the players had been double-crossed and, finding out that their promised money wasn't forthcoming, had gone out to win and put it to the gamblers; gamblers had double-crossed other gamblers and gotten to the Reds; players were double-crossing other players, and on and on, ad nauseam. One story making the rounds had one New York gambler who was not in on the fix, and had lost his bundle in games one and two, covering the fixed money in game three after finding out Kerr was not in on the conspiracy. He was said to have won over $50,000 of the fixers' money.

The White Sox win in game three began to bring a sense of sanity back to the Series. Now maybe, thought the serious Series watchers, the Series would revert to form.

But whatever measure of sanity Kerr's win brought momentarily disappeared the very next day when Cicotte went back to the mound for game four. Confiding to a fellow plotter, "We've got to look good in losing. We've got to think of our [1920] contracts," Cicotte chose an even more imaginative manner of losing this one than he had shown in game one. This time, even with a five-hitter, Cicotte lost, courtesy of two fielding mistakes he made in the fourth inning, giving the Reds two runs and a 2–0 victory. Retiring Roush to start the fifth, Cicotte got Reds' catcher Pat Duncan to tap weakly back to the mound. After inspecting the stitches on the ball, Cicotte promptly threw the ball into the stands, allowing Duncan to go to second. The next batter, Larry Kopf, singled to left in front of the oncoming left fielder, Joe Jackson. Jackson fielded the ball cleanly on the first bounce. Duncan, not wanting to challenge the best arm on the Sox, stopped at third. But now Cicotte employed a little self-help. Positioning himself directly on a line between the oncoming throw and catcher Ray Schalk, Cicotte managed to deflect the ball with his glove, pushing it into foul territory and allowing Duncan to score. The next batter, Neale, doubled, scoring Kopf, and the Reds had two runs and their third victory in the Series. Later—much later—Cicotte was to reveal that "I deliberately intercepted a throw from the outfield to the plate which might have cut off a run. At another point in the same game I purposely made a wild throw. All the runs scored against me were due to my own errors." Cicotte had done his job well. Now it was Williams's turn again in the fifth game.

Lefty Williams matched Cicotte's virtuoso performance, giving up just four hits, and four runs—again, all in one inning. After walking Morrie Rath to lead off the game, and giving the gamblers their "signal" that today was to be their day, Williams allowed just two other base runners going into the sixth, one on Risberg's error and one on Kopf's legitimate single to right center in the fifth. But in the sixth he started to groove the ball, knowing he had to protect his investment: "I was supposed to get $10,000 after the second game when we got back to Chicago, but I did not get it until after the fourth game." Williams gave up a double to the opposing pitcher, Eller, who moved to third on Felsch's wild throw. Morrie Rath then brought him in with a single. Heinie Groh walked—Williams's eighth walk in thirteen innings—and Edd Roush cleared the bases with a triple to deep center. One sacrifice fly later the Reds had their four runs and a 5–0 victory, the other run coming off Erskine Mayer, Williams's reliever. But Williams had done *his* job and the Reds had a 4–1 lead in the best-of-nine Series.

The next day Dickie Kerr came back to win Chicago's—and his—second game of the Series, 5–4 in extra innings. And in game seven Cicotte, now determined to make up for his two "thrown" games, assuaged the suspicions of manager Gleason and, with the starting assignment in hand, went out and pitched a seven-hitter to win 4–1.

All of a sudden the Series was 4–3, Cincinnati, and the highly touted Sox had a chance to even things up—even win —if Williams could match Cicotte's performance in game eight. But any hopes that Williams had changed his ways were dispelled in the first inning. In fact, two writers who had to make use of the facilities under the stands in Redland Field overheard two gamblers talking, one of whom commented, "It'll be all over in the first inning!" It was, as Williams faced but five men, giving up two singles, two doubles and three runs. Manager Gleason, sensing that Williams had not repented as had Cicotte, took him out after one-third of an inning. But it was too late. The Reds scored four runs in the first

and went on to win the game 10–5 and the Series, 5–3.

The 1920 edition of *Spalding's Official Baseball Record* summed up the 1919 Series thusly: "There is very little question that the playing ability of the Chicago team was overestimated in 1919. . . . The strength of National League clubs in 1919 was always underestimated, as was the ability of National League players individually. . . . It is not out of place to call attention to these facts, because in some quarters the defeat of the American League has been subject to criticism, which does not seem to be warranted."

Others concurred. Al Spink of *The Sporting News* was to write: "The managing editor asked me what I thought of the rumors of crookedness. . . . I replied that the talk of the selling out of certain players was pure buncombe, that there was not enough money in all the world to buy up the contenders on either side in a world's championship baseball series."

But, as the revelations which came just before the close of the 1920 season were to prove, there *was* enough money. And sadly enough, when everything had been said and done, the greatest spectacle in sports had been dishonestly played.

The Reds might have won the 1919 World Series, but the real losers were not the Chicago White Sox; they were baseball and those who believed in the sport. Nelson Algren, then a little boy living in Chicago, and one of those taken in by the dishonesty of eight men, said it all when he wrote: "Benedict Arnolds. Betrayers of American Boyhood, not to mention American Girlhood and American Womanhood and American Hoodhood."

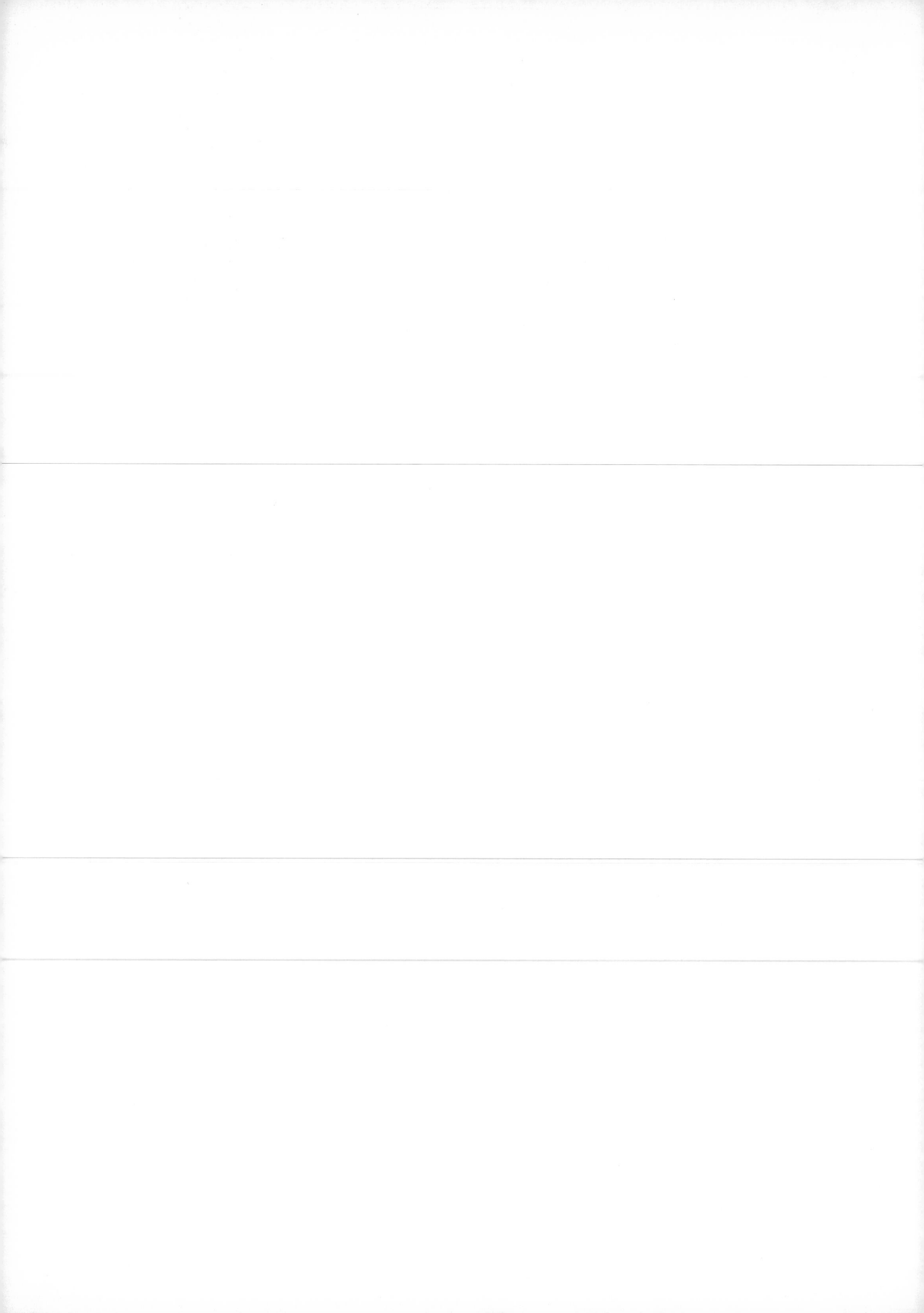

GOLDEN JUBILEE
CINCINNATI REDS
Champions 1869-1919
OFFICIAL SOUVENIR SCORE CARD.

WORLD'S SERIES
GAMES

REDLAND FIELD
1919

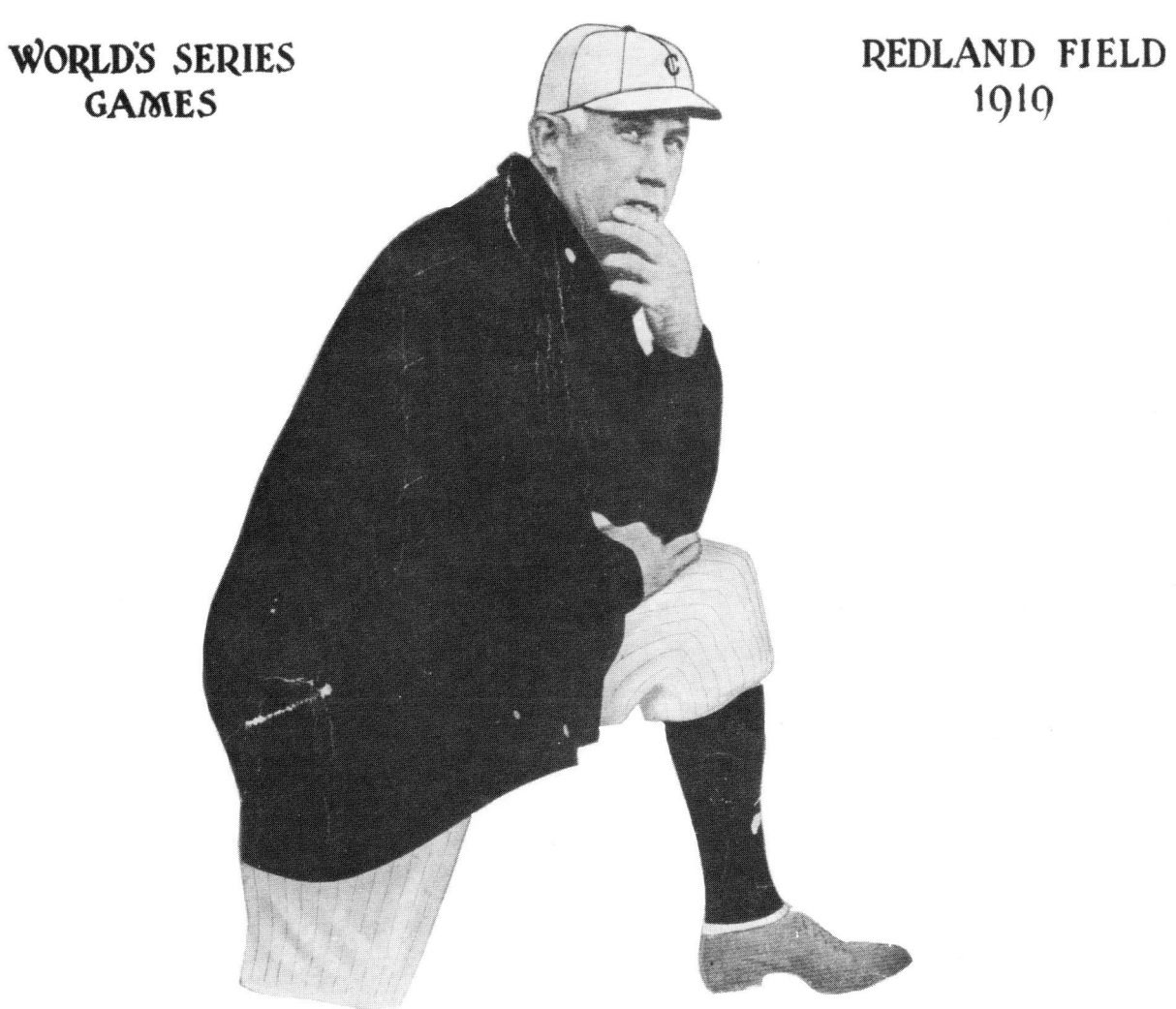

Price, 25 Cents

78

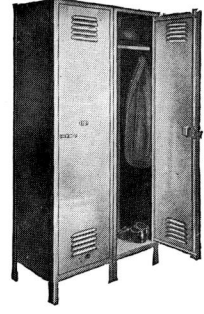
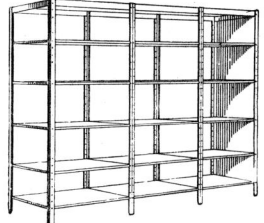

THE CINCINNATI BASE BALL CLUB COMPANY

W. J. FRIEDLANDER
VICE PRES.

C. J. Mc DIARMID
SECRETARY

AUG. HERRMANN
PRESIDENT

LOUIS C. WIDRIG
TREASURER

JAMES P. ORR

OFFICERS AND DIRECTORS

We Can't All Win a Pennant

But it is some satisfaction to see the glorious, fighting, dashing REDS—with the spirit of '69—and guided by the crafty Moran with his indomitable spirit—represent Cincinnati and her tens of thousands of base ball enthusiasts in this year's classic.

We can, however, win the admiration and respect of our friends by laying aside a small sum of money each week, thus fortifying ourselves against unexpected happenings.

The Provident Extends a Very Helpful Service to Those Desirous of Opening a Savings Account.

We add 3% interest, compounded every six months. When money is deposited on or before the 10th of the month, we start the interest from the first of the month.

The PROVIDENT SAVINGS BANK & TRUST CO.

Assets Over $15,000,000.00

Seventh and Vine Streets

Member Federal Reserve Bank

BRANCHES:
Corner Melrose and McMillan (Peebles Corner), Walnut Hills

4126 Hamilton Ave., Cumminsville
3530 Warsaw Ave., Price Hill
Corner Eighth and Freeman Ave.

Patrick Joseph Moran

By JACK RYDER, Sporting Editor Cincinnati Enquirer

FIVE years ago there were three cities in the National League which had never enjoyed the sporting delight of supporting a pennant-winning baseball team. Today there is only one such disconsolate community.

For forty years the Philadelphia Club was immersed in the second division, but in Nineteen Hundred and Fifteen Sleeptown gladly and uproariously celebrated the winning of its first National League flag.

For fifty barren seasons the Redland rooters consoled themselves with the glorious history of the Reds of Sixty-Nine, while their modern representatives floundered through one disappointing season after another. Today the banner of victory flies over Redland Field, and three hundred thousand eager fans are trying to crowd their way into the park to see the struggle for the championship of the baseball world.

Thus has Patrick Joseph Moran brought joy and brightness into the lives of the citizens of two great commonwealths. For it was Pat who assumed control of a disregarded club four years ago and astonished the nation by guiding his overlooked team to a brilliant championship.

And now he has transferred his genial personality and his unquestioned ability to the Queen City of the West, and has placed Cincinnati upon the glittering pinnacle of baseball fame. He has worked patiently and skilfully with a baseball club which was not considered as a pennant possibility six months ago, and now he leads his winners to the field to battle for the world's greatest honors.

In these moments of delirious happiness it is proper that a silent tear be shed over the sorrowful fate of St. Louis, the one remaining city in the league which has never harbored a winning club. For Patrick J. Moran will never lift the Mound City from its depths of dark despair.

He has reached the end of his journeyings. This kindly, liberal, patient, industrious and intelligent Irishman is here to stay.

Hats off to Pat, the pennant maker!

CONCENTRATED EFFORT

PUT PAT. MORAN'S REDS TO THE FORE IN FANDOM AND HAS

MADE THE HOTEL HAVLIN

— AND —

HOTEL METROPOLE SERVICE

FAMOUS AMONG THE TRAVELING PUBLIC.

GEO. W. MARTIN, GEN'L MANAGER

Will it be Another 50 Years?

By TOM SWOPE, Sporting Editor, Cincinnati Post

THIS, as the cover of this program tells you, is Cincinnati's golden jubilee year in baseball. This is the fiftieth anniversary of the Reds of 1869 who never lost a game.

And on this fiftieth anniversary year of that great team Cincinnati again is celebrating the triumph of another championship club—the team that won the first pennant Cincinnati ever captured in the National League.

Will it be another 50 years before Cincinnati again celebrates the winning of a pennant?

Will many of us who are gathered here for the world series games be dead and buried years before Cincinnati again tops the heap? I think not.

Instead I expect to see Cincinnati engaging in another world series or two within the next five years.

Now that Cincinnati has won a pennant she is just getting started. The Reds of Pat Moran are not a bloomer team that will fade out of the picture next year.

Pat has a club that is built to last a long time. He'll only need to put on a new part here and a new part there to keep his machine running like a well-oiled clock for several years more.

And some of the new parts which may be needed now are decorating the Red bench or are owned by the Cincinnati Club and are gaining the necessary experience out in the minors.

There's no reason Cincinnati should stop, now that the ice has been broken and the first flag won.

Redland is in the pennant swim. The water's fine and there is no reason for getting out of the big doings.

Huskiness, Hustle and Harmony

By BOB NEWHALL, Sporting Editor, Commercial Tribune

JUST as the famous Three R's—Readin', Ritin' and Rithmetic—has formed the backbone of many a brilliant career, so have the Three H's—Huskiness, Hustle and Harmony—done equally as much for the Reds of 1919.

As to the first—Huskiness—this lies not solely in avoirdupois and bulk of sinew, but in the preparing and keeping of such thews and muscles as one is endowed, in the very pink of condition. And that is what these Redland champions have done, from the first game in April up until the present great occasion that has caused this program and this screed to be brought into being. There have been no joy-rides, no giving the wine when it is red the once over and the twice across, no athletes climbing to echoing boudoirs by way of the fire-escape. Everybody has kept his body as he has been paid to keep it—always ready to give his club and his management the best it is capable of.

The second item—Hustle—has been a watchword with this team of dope-upsetters as it has always been the watchword of every team Pat Moran has had anything to do with. They hustle in their practice, they hustle to the field, and they hustle back to the bat. All the grass that could possibly grow under their collective feet wouldn't dry into enough hay to start a fire. They hustle out infield taps that seem sure outs, they hustle to the coaching lines to cheer their toiling brethren on, and it is even said, on fairly good authority, that they hustle to their meals!

Third and last of this triumvirate of Red success-makers—Harmony—is far from least. They live, not as brothers—for any crowd of brothers we have ever seen get along like strange bulldogs—but as good friends, say. They seek not secluded corners alone to sulk in their several tents like the Arabs, nursing grudges. But in cheery groups and sometimes in flocks they hunt the marts of amusement, arms locked, slaps on backs frequent, merry jibe and jest bandied back and forth. And the results of all this is shown clearly on the ball field. For when one man hates another and throws a ball to him, he may hope he catches it for the good of the team, but he also hopes that if it is to be Fate that that ball be muffed, it will knock three teeth out or at least close an eye!

How the Flag was Won

By W. A. PHELON, Sporting Editor Cincinnati Times-Star

ON the evidence of the official records, the Reds won out because they were the best ball club. They did the best and most effective hitting, they outfielded the other seven clubs, and their pitching was of the classiest pattern. All well and good—but the final triumph came because each department co-ordinated with the others. The pitchers couldn't have won but for the fielding back of them—and the pitching and fielding, combined, wouldn't have been so much if the club hadn't done the hitting at the time of need.

Few clubs, in many seasons, have shown such even balance of the different departments as the Reds. There has been beautifully perfect machine-work all along the line. If you don't believe it, ask the Giants. They know. The pitching—which, before the season, was picked as specially weak—has not only been superb, but has been almost equally divided among the husky flingers. The catching has been smooth and thoroughly effective. Before the campaign began, it was said that the Red infield was shaky and unreliable. There isn't another infield, in either league, which has shown more class, more steadiness, more speed and all-round skill—and no infield which has a better total batting average.

The outfielding has been of topnotch quality, even during the dark days when left field was filled by gallant volunteers—the time when Rube Bressler came to the rescue and showed such speed that the club fought along successfully till Sherwood Magee recovered his health and reinforcements came in the shape of Duncan and See. Taken as a whole, the defensive work of the Reds has been the best in the league—an average of little more than one error per game all season.

By sticking to their knitting, playing steady, earnest baseball all the time, the Reds surprised the rest of the league by moving to the front in mid-summer—but the decisive games, the battles that really ended all discussion, were played at New York in August. The Reds came into New York to play six games in three days—a tremendous task against a great ball club headed by a wizard manager. And when the Reds left New York, they left the gallant Giants wondering how the explosion happened, while the wizard manager, both hands upon his aching brow, was acknowledging he had met a faster, better ball club than his own. Those games in New York settled the championship. Around August 1, there were only two clubs in the race. After August 15, there was only one club in the procession. That club had earned its honors by clean and speedy ball playing, by perfect co-operation under a great leader—and by the glorious victories gained on the Polo Grounds.

It's a club where every man is a star, but where the stars all shine together. And that's why they won the flag.

Champion Reds of 1869

Cincinnati's Champions of 1882

By REN MULFORD, Jr.

SOME years after the famed '69 Reds had completed their triumphal tour of the country, the National League was born. Cincinnati, cradle of the professional game, was one of the eight original members of the parent body in 1876. The Reds trailed that year, finishing last. They repeated the disaster in 1877, and were then bounced for non-payment of dues. Reinstated they came within gunshot of winning a championship in 1878, finishing second to Boston. In '79 they dropped to fifth place, and 1880 once more found them a bad last and they dropped down and out of the game.

During 1881 Cincinnati was without professional representation in any organization, but during that winter at the old Gibson House the American Association came into the field. The new baby of balldom thrived, although the old National League eyed it with its fingers crossed. Under the captaincy of Charles N. Snyder, the Reds of '82 revived in some degree the old flame of enthusiasm and brought to Cincinnati her first baseball championship.

There were only two pitchers on the '82 staff—Will H. White, the spectacled forerunner of Lee Meadows of today, and Harry McCormick. It was no trick in those days for pitchers to work in successive games, and White pitched 54 and McCormick 25 of the season's allotment. Captain Snyder caught in 70 of the 80 games that were played, and Phil Powers in the few that were left.

On the infield Harry Luff played in the beginning. He was only hitting at a .241 clip when Danny Stearns was enlisted and he put the steam of a .302 average behind his drives. John A. McPhee ("King Bid") was on second; "Old Hickory" W. W. Carpenter played third, and Charley Fulmer at short. With two native sons—Joe Sommer in left and Harry Wheeler in right and Jimmy Macullar in center, the new Reds set a lively pace. They led the Association in hitting, with a team average of .266 and were the fielding leaders, excelling with an average of .912. Cincinnati finished far ahead of her nearest and liveliest rival—the Eclipse team of Louisville. This first Red championship was clinched with 54 games won and 26 lost, a percentage of .675 to .555, the credit of the Kentucky second-placers. The other clubs in the fight were the Athletics of Philadelphia, Allegheny, St. Louis and Baltimore. President A. S. Stern, of the winning Reds, gave them a banquet at the old St. Nicholas, but rain spoiled the benefit game planned by the populace and only 1,000 turned out. The Reds did harvest a little extra coin and glory by defeating the Chicago White Stockings, and Captain Anson, 4 to 0. The next day the National League Champions turned the scale and whitewashed the Reds 2 to 0. These were among the most exciting games ever played on the old Bank Street grounds. They were witnessed by about 7,000 early fans, and were really the curtain raisers to the World's Series, now the Great Classic of the National Game.

CINCINNATI REDS, CHAMPIONS 1882, AMERICAN ASSOCIATION
Top Row, Standing (Left to Right)—McCormick, p.; Powers, c.; Stearns, 1st b.; McPhee, 2nd b.   Middle Row, Sitting (Left to Right)—Carpenter, 3rd b.; Snyder, c.; White, p.; Fulmer, ss.; Sommer, l. f.   Bottom Row, Sitting (Left to Right)—Macullar, c. f.; Wheeler, r. f.

A Bit of Redland History and a Personal Tribute

By REN MULFORD, Jr.

WAY back in the troublous days during the fourth of the baseball wars, Cincinnati, although outside the direct line of clash of National and American League rivalry, was a storm-center of discontent. John T. Brush, then the head of Red administration, was the target for intermittent attack. Day after day interests unfriendly to the National League were busy as nailers in print. They opened up streets through Redland Field. They sold the Cincinnati Club to many other people. It was a day of "great doings"—in the headlines. Redland was a melting pot of rumor.

It was during the Reds' trip to St. Louis in the early summer of 1902 that Frank Bancroft said to me: "I don't know how much truth there is in all this talk of John T. getting out, but I hear that if he really wants to sell that Garry Herrmann, Geo. B. Cox and Julius Fleischmann will take the Red Club off his hands."

That was one rumor that had not seen the light of print. A week later, on my way to catch the midnight limited for Boston, I ran into the very same rumor on Broadway in New York.

The Enquirer had not indulged in any of these speculative dreams of changed ownership, but here was old Dame Rumor peddling the same yarn in New York that I'd heard in St. Louis.

It was a case of hurried back-pedaling to the Enquirer Bureau. The story of three new Richmonds in the field, ready to take the Red Club off the hands of the old owners, was quickly written and sent out to Redland. It was a story that changed Cincinnati's baseball history.

"I am not responsible for this article," is about what Garry Herrmann wrote to John T. Brush in enclosing the Enquirer clipping, "but if the Cincinnati Baseball Club is for sale, we will make the story good—we will buy the club."

And that was the beginning of the deal that now is happily culminating in the greatest championship honors ever won by a Cincinnati team. Garry Herrmann brought a new spirit of fairness and sanity into baseball. National and American Leagues were grappling at each other's throats. The game itself was suffering. It took a master mind to bring order out of chaos. Peace did not come in a day, but the leaven of common sense of the Garry Herrmann brand was at work in receptive minds.

Baseball has had many heroic figures who deserve the high places that have been accorded them in diamond history. William H. Hulbert is one of the figures that stands out prominently—the man who put baseball on its everlasting foundation of rugged honesty. Cincinnati may well be proud of Garry Herrmann, who, as chairman of the National Commission, is accorded a seat among Balldom's mighty. He well deserves the title bestowed upon him years ago as the Chief Justice of the Supreme Court of Baseball.

We old Redbugs can remember the red fire and the cheers with which Garry Herrmann and the Red Administration of 1903 were acclaimed. In this year of 1919 is fulfilled all the hopes and dreams of every subsequent year of struggle for the championship, which now belongs to Pat Moran and his Battling Redlegs.

"Time Hill," Cincinnati
and four examples
of its fine watches

"Time Hill" is the result of the happy combination of Swiss skill and American Industry.

It makes possible the beautiful Gruen watches, famous among horologists for their precision timekeeping.

Made in Madre-Biel, Switzerland, by a Guild of the best craftsmen, equipped with the most modern machinery under American ownership and direction, the movements are brought to the Guild Workshops at "Time Hill," Cincinnati, shown above, where they are adjusted and timed in *beautiful, hand-wrought Gruen cases.*

When you own a watch with the name "Gruen" on the dial, you own a fine modern example of Swiss watchmaking—with the complete service of this American "Time Hill" Workshop behind it.

Gruen watches for every purpose and in many styles are sold by 1200 Jeweler Agencies, the best in every locality, to whom the sale is confined.

GRUEN WATCHMAKERS' GUILD
Makers of the famous Gruen Watches since 1874
"Time Hill," Iowa Street, Cincinnati, Ohio

THE OLD WAY   VERITHIN WAY

How the Pat. Gruen wheel train construction made an accurate watch thin. The shortness of staff makes watch more durable.

Highest timekeeping perfection attained in movements marked "Precision."

The "Hexagon" Wristlet . . . . . $ 65 to $ 85
Set with full cut AA1 Diamonds : . . . 100 to 400

GRUEN VERITHIN AND WRIST WATCHES

16

1869

Member
Champion
Reds,
1869

1919

GEORGE WRIGHT

Reds of 1919 — Champions National League

Patrick Moran
Manager
Born at Fitchburg, Mass., February 7, 1876. Started playing ball in 1895 with Athol, Mass. With Montreal in 1899 and 1900. With Boston Nationals from 1901 to 1905. With Chicago Nationals from 1906 to 1909. With Philadelphia Nationals from 1910 to 1918. Made Manager in 1915 and won the pennant for Philadelphia in 1915. Came to Cincinnati in 1919

Harry F. Sallee
Pitcher
Born in Higginsport, Ohio, February 3, 1885. Began playing with the Meridian Club in 1905. Purchased by New York Americans in 1907 and released. Joined the St. Louis Nationals where he remained eight years. In 1916 he was sold to the New York Giants. Secured by the Reds in 1919.

Walter H. Ruether
Pitcher
Born in 1893. Played with Pittsburgh Nationals in 1913 then to Los Angeles, Sacramento, Vancouver, Salt Lake, Spokane and Portland. Joined Chicago Cubs in 1917 and sold to Cincinnati that year. Joined the army and returned to the Reds in 1919.

Henry Groh
Captain and Third Base
Born at Rochester, N. Y., September 18, 1889. Lives in Cincinnati. Started playing with the University of Rochester in 1907. Then played three years with Oshkosh, Wis. In 1911 was with Decatur, then went to New York and remained with the Giants until 1913 when he came to Cincinnati and has played here since.

Reds of 1919 — Champions National League

Horace A. Eller
Pitcher

Born in Muncie, Ind., in 1894. Lives at Danville, Ill. Started playing with the Champaign Club in 1913 and played one year with Danville and two years with Moline. Joined the Reds in 1917.

James J. Ring
Pitcher

Born in Brooklyn in 1895. Started playing with the Brooklyn Nationals. Was sent to Jersey City in 1915. With Utica in 1916 and came to Cincinnati in 1917, in which year he was sent to Buffalo and returned to Cincinnati in 1918.

Ray L. Fisher
Pitcher

Born in Middleburg, Vt., October 4, 1887. Played with the Hartford Club in 1908 and 1909 when he was sold to the New York Americans. Played nine years with the Yankees and then was purchased by the Cincinnati Club.

Raymond Bressler
Pitcher

Born in Brookville, Pa., October 23, 1895. Lives in Flemington, Pa. First played with the Harrisburg Club. Then three years with the Philadelphia Americans. Then to Atlanta and came to Cincinnati in 1918. Joined the army but returned to the Reds in 1919.

CINCINNATI	1	2	3	4	5	6	7	8	9	10	A.B.	R.	I.B.	S.H.	P.O.	A.	E.
1-Rath, 2 b																	
2-Daubert, 1 b																	
3-Groh, 3 b																	
4-Roush, c f																	
5-Duncan, l f																	
6-Kopf, s s																	
7-Neale, r f																	
8-Wingo, c 9-Rariden, c 10-Allen, c																	
11-Sallee, p 12-Reuther, p																	
13-Eller, p 14-Ring, p																	

PITCHERS
15-Fisher
16-Luque
17-Gerner
18-Bressler
19-Mitchell

INFIELDERS
20-Smith
21-Schreiber

OUTFIELDERS
22-See
23-Magee

Two-Base Hits..............Three-Base Hits.............Home Run.............Passed Balls.............Wild Pitches............
Bases on Hit by Pitched Ball...........Struck Out.........Left on Bases.........Double Plays..........Bases on Balls..........

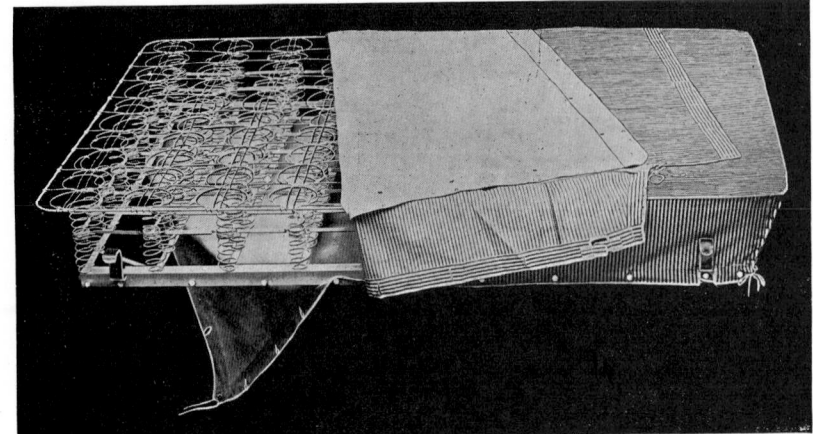

Chicago
White Sox

———

Champions
American League

———

1919

Photo copyright by F. P. Burke, Chicago.

TOP ROW, LEFT TO RIGHT

R. Wilkinson ....Pitcher
H. McClellan ....Infield
W. Sullivan ....Pitcher
G. Loudermilk ....Pitcher
B. Lynn ....Catcher
C. Gandil ....Infield
H. Liebold ....Outfield
F. McMullen ....Infield
Ed. Murphy ....Outfield
Ed. Cicotte ....Pitcher
C. Risberg ....Infield
U. Faber ....Pitcher

BOTTOM ROW, LEFT TO RIGHT

Ray Schalk ....Catcher
J. Jenkins ....Catcher
R. Kerr ....Pitcher
J. Collins ....Outfield
J. Mayer ....Pitcher
W. Gleason ....Manager
C. Williams ....Pitcher
E. Collins ....Infield
G. Weaver ....Infield
O. Felsch ....Outfield
Joe Jackson ....Outfield
W. James ....Pitcher
Sharkey............Club House Boy

CHICAGO:	1	2	3	4	5	6	7	8	9	10	A.B.	R.	I.B.	S.H.	P.O.	A.	E.	
1-Leibold, r f																		PITCHERS
2-E. Collins, 2 b																		13-Faber
3-Weaver, 3 b																		14-Williams
4-Jackson, l f																		15-Sullivan
5-Felsch, c f																		16-Wilkinson
6-Gandil, 1 b																		17-Mayer
7-Risberg, s s																		CATCHERS
8-Schalk, c																		18-Jenkins
9-Cicott, p / 10-Kerr, p																		19-Lynn
11-James, p / 12-Loudermilk, p																		INFIELDERS
																		20-McMullin
																		21-McClellan
																		OUTFIELDERS
																		22-Murphy
																		23-J. Collins

Two-Base Hits................Three-Base Hits............Home Runs.............Passed Balls............Wild Pitches............
Bases on Hit by Pitched Ball..........Struck Out.........Left on Bases.........Double Plays.........Bases on Balls..........

Reds of 1919 — Champions National League

Jacob E. Daubert
First Base

Born in Shamokin, Pa., April 17, 1886. Lives in Schuylkill Haven, Pa. Began playing with the Kane, Pa., Club in 1907. With Cleveland in 1908 and Toledo for two years. Joined the Brooklyn Club in 1910 and remained there until this season.

Morris G. Rath
Second Base

Born in Mobeetie, Texas, December 25, 1887. Now lives in Philadelphia. Started playing ball with Wilmington, N. C., then with Reading, Philadelphia Americans, Baltimore, Chicago Americans, Kansas City, Toronto, and Salt Lake City. Joined the Navy in 1918 and last spring signed with the Reds.

Wm. Larry Kopf
Short Stop

Born in Bristol, Conn., in 1893 and started playing ball with Fordham University in 1909. Then with Cleveland, Toledo, Philadelphia Americans and Baltimore. With the Reds in 1917 and in the Army in 1918, returning to the Reds in 1919.

Henry W. Schreiber
Utility Infielder

Born in Cleveland, Ohio, July 12, 1893. Started playing with Duluth in 1913. Then with the Chicago White Sox and to Lincoln for two years. In 1917 joined the Boston Nationals and went to war the same year. Was secured by the Reds this year from Waterbury, Conn.

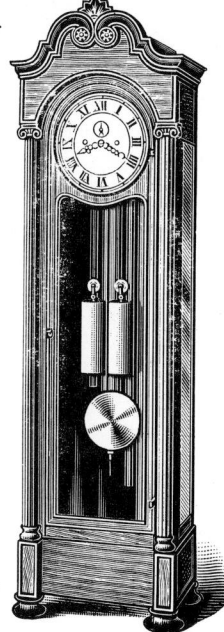

Reds of 1919—Champions National League

Ivy B. Wingo
Catcher
Born in Norcross, Ga., in 1890. Started playing at Greenville, S. C., in 1909. Then to the St. Louis Nationals and remained until 1914, when he signed with the Reds and has been here since.

William A. Rariden
Catcher
Born in Bedford, Ind., February 5, 1888. Started playing at Canton, O., in 1907. Joined Boston Nationals in 1909 and remained 5 years. Played with the Indianapolis and Newark Federals in 1915. With the New York Giants for the next three years. Secured by Cincinnati last fall.

Roy A. Mitchell
Pitcher
Born in Texas, April 19, 1895. Still lives there. Started playing ball in 1908 with San Antonio. Then to Ft. Worth. Then to Houston in 1910. Then to St. Louis Americans, where he remained five years. Then with the Vernon (California) Club, coming to Cincinnati in 1918.

Nick Allen
Catcher
Born in Norton, Kan., 1892. Lives at Udall, Kan. Started playing at Wichita in 1910. With Chicago White Sox 1911. With Minneapolis for the next two years. Then with the Chicago Cubs and Topeka in 1916 and Providence 1917. Then secured by the Reds but went into the army. At the close of the war rejoined the Reds.

Chas. A. Comiskey
(The Old Roman)
President, Chicago "White Sox"

F. C. Bancroft
(The Old War Horse)
Business Manager, Cincinnati Reds

Reds of 1919—Champions National League

Earle Neale
Right Field
Born at Parkersburg, W. Va., November 16, 1892. Still lives there. Started playing with the London (Ont.) Club in 1912. Then played with Cleveland, Saginaw and Wheeling. Was secured by the Reds in 1915 and has since played here.

Edward Roush
Center Field
Born in Oakland City, Ind., May 8, 1893. Still lives there. Started playing at Evansville in 1912. With the Indianapolis Federals for two years. Then with Newark, N. J. With the New York Giants in 1916 and traded to the Reds that year.

Sherwood Magee
Left Field.
Born at Clarendon, Pa., August 6, 1884. Lives in Philadelphia. Was with Philadelphia Nationals from 1904 to 1915. With Boston Nationals from 1915 to 1917 when he was secured by the Reds.

Louis B. Duncan
Left Field
Born at Coalton, Ohio, October 6. 1893. Lives at Vincennes, Ind. Started playing in 1913 with Flint, Mich. Then with Battlecreek, Grand Rapids and Birmingham. He was purchased recently by the Reds from the Birmingham Club.

*You Can
See it From
Redland Field*

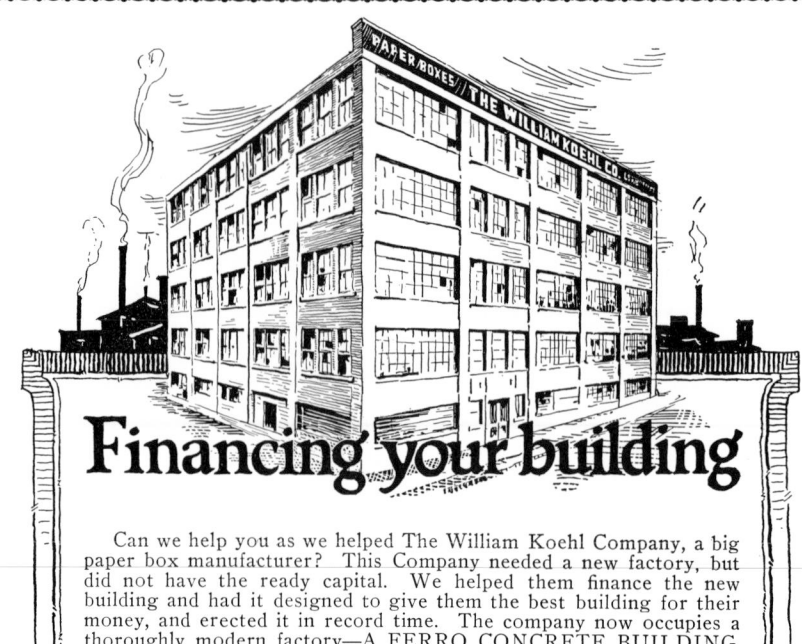

Financing your building

Can we help you as we helped The William Koehl Company, a big paper box manufacturer? This Company needed a new factory, but did not have the ready capital. We helped them finance the new building and had it designed to give them the best building for their money, and erected it in record time. The company now occupies a thoroughly modern factory—A FERRO CONCRETE BUILDING. In this new structure it manufactures under conditions which leave nothing to be desired that makes for low cost of production and contented employes.

While in Cincinnati, call at our Office, Richmond and Harriet Streets, or telephone West 4180 and we will be glad to show you through some of the buildings erected by us.

The "Store of Style Without Extravagance"

Is the Store for Everybody!

—*The Store for Young Men—Older Men—and Boys*—because their Shop is conveniently located on the Main Floor at West Entrance and can be entered directly. No need to pass through any of the Departments for Women. Moreover, the salespeople are experts, and can help you to select what is best for your individual needs.

—*The Store for Women of Fashion* because they can obtain the new things here as soon as they are launched in New York, the country's greatest Fashion Center. Here, too, is where they bring their daughters, large and small—to the store where they can clothe them correctly at the least expenditure of money and energy, because our Departments are so arranged that all ready-to-wear merchandise is on the same floor.

The McAlpin Store

BODE

Truck Bodies

One or a Thousand   **Custom Made**

Cincinnati

Reds of 1919—Champions National League

Edward F. Gerner
Pitcher
Born in Philadelphia, July 22, 1897. Played in Albany in 1915 and Reading 1916. Was secured by the Reds in 1917.

James L. Smith
Utility Infielder
Born at Pittsburg. First played with Chicago Federals, then with the Pittsburg Nationals, Toronto, New York Giants and Boston Nationals, and joined the Reds last spring.

Adolfo Luque
Pitcher
Born in Havana, Cuba, August 4, 1890. Played amateur ball in Cuba until 1912. Then joined the Long Branch, N. J., Club. Played with the Boston Nationals in 1914. Then with Toronto and Louisville. Purchased from the Louisville Club by Cincinnati in 1918.

Charles H. See
Utility Outfielder
Born in Pleasantville, N. Y., October 13, 1897. His only professional ball playing previous to joining the Reds, some months ago, was with the Rochester Club of the International League.

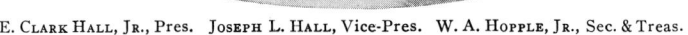

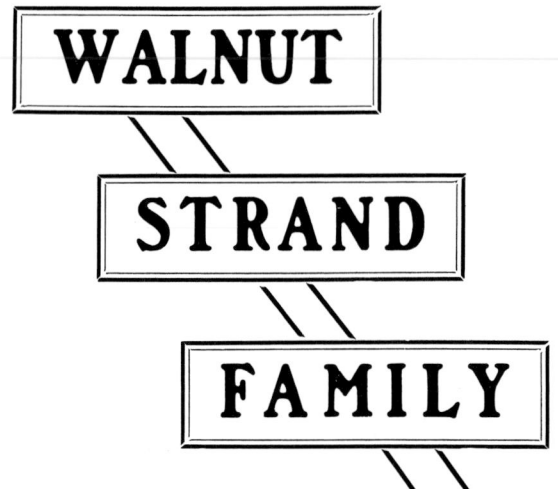

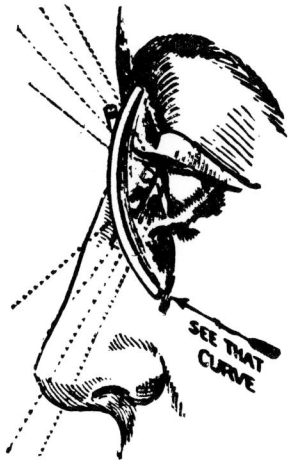
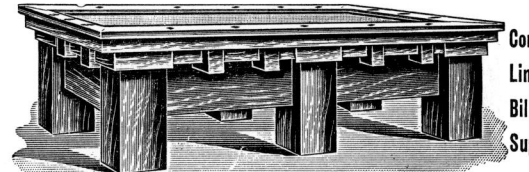

REDLAND FIELD NATIONAL LEAGUE CINCINNATI

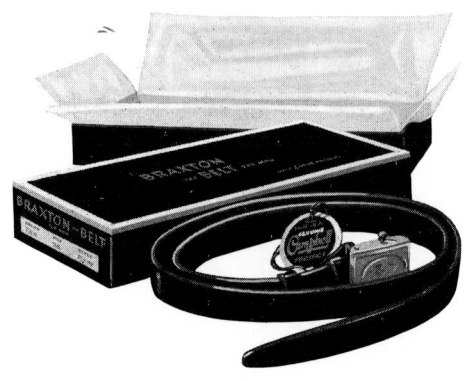

The National Commission

B. B. Johnson	Aug. Herrmann	John A. Heydler
President	Chairman	President
American League		National League

RULES AND REGULATIONS GOVERNING THE CONTESTS FOR THE PROFESSIONAL BASEBALL CHAMPIONSHIP OF THE WORLD

Agreement to Play

Section 1.   The pennant-winning club of the National League and the pennant-winning club of the American League shall meet annually in a series of games for the Professional Baseball Championship of the World.

To Be Played Under Supervision of National Commission

Section 3.   The games shall be played under the supervision, control and direction of the National Commission.

*If it comes from
"Golde's" it's alright*

Style Headquarters
for
Men's Furnishings

Our tremendous outlet and
unlimited buying power not only
keep us in intimate relationship with Style
Centers but also enable us to display the
ultra-fashionable creations at the same time that
leading Specialty Shops of the East show them.

Shirts
Neckwear
Underwear
Hosiery
Novelties

—Such as Gentlemen prefer and at prices
surprisingly moderate.

Visitors—

Are always welcome. There is a
"Golde" Store near your hotel.

Geo.
Golde
& Co.

Cincinnati's Largest Distributors of Men's Furnishings

*Assets
Over
One Hundred
and
Twenty-Eight
Million Dollars*

*Cincinnati's
Largest
and Ohio's
Largest
Financial
Institution*

**THE UNION CENTRAL LIFE BUILDING
CINCINNATI**

Two Years Before the Cincinnati Red Stockings Made Their Famous Record in 1869, The Union Central Life Insurance Company Was Established

From a small beginning it has grown until now it has life insurance policies in force insuring over five hundred and sixty-three million dollars. It is engaged in business in forty-six States and is helping to make Cincinnati famous far and wide, because of its remarkable record and its generous treatment of policy holders. The name Union Central Life, in the minds of tens of thousands throughout the United States, stands for "low cost" and "service."

Communicate today with one of the Union Central representatives.

THE UNION CENTRAL LIFE INSURANCE CO.

JESSE R. CLARK, President

JOHN L. SHUFF, Manager Home Office General Agency   **CHARLES J. STERN, General Agent**

1926

St. Louis Cardinals
vs.
New York Yankees

1926 WORLD SERIES COMPOSITE BOX

	Wins	Composite Line Score
St. Louis Cardinals (N.L.)	4	5 0 2 10 2 0 9 0 3 0 – 31
New York Yankees (A.L.)	3	2 2 2 2 4 5 2 0 1 1 – 21

Manager	Regular Season W	L	Pct.	G. Ahead
Rogers Hornsby	89	65	.578	2
Miller Huggins	91	63	.591	3

BATTING AND FIELDING

ST. LOUIS CARDINALS

WORLD SERIES STATISTICS

	Pos	G	AB	R	H	2B	3B	HR	RBI	BB	SO	SB	BA	SA	PO	A	E
Jim Bottomley	1b	7	29	4	10	3	0	0	5	1	2	0	.345	.448	79	1	0
Rogers Hornsby	2b	7	28	2	7	1	0	0	4	2	2	1	.250	.286	15	21	0
Tommy Thevenow	ss	7	24	5	10	1	0	1	4	0	1	0	.417	.583	10	26	2
Les Bell	3b	7	27	4	7	1	0	1	6	2	5	0	.259	.407	7	17	2
Billy Southworth	rf	7	29	6	10	1	1	1	4	0	0	1	.345	.552	8	3	0
Taylor Douthit	cf	4	15	3	4	2	0	0	1	3	2	0	.267	.400	4	2	0
Chick Hafey	lf	7	27	2	5	2	0	0	0	0	7	0	.185	.259	21	1	0
Bob O'Farrell	c	7	23	2	7	1	0	0	2	2	2	0	.304	.348	35	8	0
Wattie Holm	ph-rf-cf	5	16	1	2	0	0	0	1	1	2	0	.125	.125	7	0	0
Jake Flowers	ph	3	3	0	0	0	0	0	0	0	1	0	.000	.000			
Specs Toporcer	ph	1	0	0	0	0	0	0	1	0	0	0	—	—			
Ray Blades		Did not play-injured															
Ernie Vick		Did not play															
Pete Alexander	p	3	7	1	0	0	0	0	0	0	2	0	.000	.000	0	6	1
Bill Sherdel	p	2	5	0	0	0	0	0	0	0	2	0	.000	.000	2	5	0
Jesse Haines	p	3	5	1	3	0	0	1	2	0	1	0	.600	1.200	0	6	0
Flint Rhem	p	1	1	0	0	0	0	0	0	0	1	0	.000	.000	0	1	0
Hi Bell	p	1	0	0	0	0	0	0	0	0	0	0	—	—	0	0	0
Wild Bill Hallahan	p	1	0	0	0	0	0	0	0	0	0	0	—	—	1	0	0
Vic Keen	p	1	0	0	0	0	0	0	0	0	0	0	—	—	0	1	0
Art Reinhart	p	1	0	0	0	0	0	0	0	0	0	0	—	—	0	0	0
Allan Sothoron		Did not play															
Syl Johnson		Did not play															
Ed Clough		Did not play															
team total		7	239	31	65	12	1	4	30	11	30	2	.272	.381	189	98	5

Double Plays–6
Left on Bases–43

REGULAR SEASON STATISTICS

		Main Pos	G	AB	R	H	2B	3B	HR	RBI	BB	SO	SB	BA	SA
Jim Bottomley		1b	154	603	98	180	40	14	19	120	58	52	4	.299	.506
Rogers Hornsby		2b	134	527	96	167	34	5	11	93	61	39	3	.317	.463
Tommy Thevenow		ss	156	563	64	144	15	5	2	63	27	26	8	.256	.311
Les Bell		3b	155	581	85	189	33	14	17	100	54	62	9	.325	.518
Billy Southworth	a	of	99	391	76	124	22	6	11	69	26	9	13	.317	.488
Taylor Douthit		of	139	530	96	163	20	4	3	52	55	46	23	.308	.377
Chick Hafey		of	78	225	30	61	19	2	4	38	11	36	2	.271	.427
Bob O'Farrell		c	147	492	63	144	30	9	7	68	61	44	1	.293	.433
Wattie Holm		of	55	144	18	41	5	1	0	21	18	14	3	.285	.333
Jake Flowers		2b	40	74	13	20	1	0	3	9	5	9	1	.270	.405
Specs Toporcer		2b	64	88	13	22	3	2	0	9	8	9	1	.250	.330
Ray Blades		of	107	416	81	127	17	12	8	43	62	57	6	.305	.462
Ernie Vick		c	24	51	6	10	2	0	0	4	3	4	0	.196	.235
Pete Alexander	b	p	23	50	1	6	1	0	0	3	2	14	0	.120	.140
Bill Sherdel		p	36	90	9	22	5	1	1	8	1	9	0	.244	.356
Jesse Haines		p	33	61	4	13	1	0	0	1	3	5	0	.213	.230
Flint Rhem		p	34	96	11	18	1	0	1	12	4	36	0	.188	.229
Hi Bell		p	27	25	3	3	0	0	0	1	3	5	0	.120	.120
Wild Bill Hallahan		p	19	16	0	4	1	0	0	0	0	7	0	.250	.313
Vic Keen		p	26	53	2	3	0	0	0	1	2	15	0	.057	.057
Art Reinhart		p	40	63	7	20	2	2	0	11	1	3	1	.317	.413
Allan Sothoron		p	15	13	2	3	0	0	0	0	1	1	0	.231	.231
Syl Johnson		p	19	12	0	0	0	0	0	0	0	5	0	.000	.000
Ed Clough		p	1	1	0	0	0	0	0	0	0	0	0	.000	.000
team total			156	5381	817	1541	259	82	90	756	478	518	83	.286	.415

a—from New York (N)
b—from Chicago (N)
Heinie Mueller (of), Jack Smith (ph), Bill Warwick (c), Eddie Dyer (p), Walter Huntzinger (p), Duster Mails (p) also played for the Cardinals during the season.

NEW YORK YANKEES

WORLD SERIES STATISTICS

	Pos	G	AB	R	H	2B	3B	HR	RBI	BB	SO	SB	BA	SA	PO	A	E
Lou Gehrig	1b	7	23	1	8	2	0	0	4	5	4	0	.348	.435	78	1	0
Tony Lazzeri	2b	7	26	2	5	1	0	0	3	1	6	0	.192	.231	15	19	1
Mark Koenig	ss	7	32	2	4	1	0	0	2	0	6	0	.125	.156	12	24	4
Joe Dugan	3b	7	24	2	8	1	0	0	2	1	1	0	.333	.375	7	14	1
Babe Ruth	rf-lf	7	20	6	6	0	0	4	5	11	2	1	.300	.900	8	2	0
Earle Combs	cf	7	28	3	10	2	0	0	2	5	2	0	.357	.429	17	0	0
Bob Meusel	lf-rf	7	21	3	5	1	1	0	0	6	1	0	.238	.381	13	0	1
Hank Severeid	c	7	22	1	6	1	0	0	1	1	2	0	.273	.318	37	7	0
Ben Paschal	ph	5	4	0	1	0	0	0	1	1	2	0	.250	.250			
Pat Collins	c	3	2	0	0	0	0	0	0	0	1	0	.000	.000	1	0	0
Mike Gazella	3b	1	0	0	0	0	0	0	0	0	0	0	—	—	1	2	0
Spence Adams	pr	2	0	0	0	0	0	0	0	0	0	0	—	—			
Benny Bengough		Did not play—shoulder injury															
Roy Carlyle		Did not play															
Aaron Ward		Did not play															
Herb Pennock	p	3	7	1	1	1	0	0	0	0	0	0	.143	.286	0	6	0
Waite Hoyt	p	2	6	0	0	0	0	0	0	0	1	0	.000	.000	0	1	0
Dutch Ruether	p-ph	3	4	0	0	0	0	0	0	0	0	0	.000	.000	0	2	0
Bob Shawkey	p	3	2	0	0	0	0	0	0	0	1	0	.000	.000	0	1	0
Urban Shocker	p	2	2	0	0	0	0	0	0	0	2	0	.000	.000	0	2	0
Myles Thomas	p	2	0	0	0	0	0	0	0	0	0	0	—	—	0	2	0
Sad Sam Jones	p	1	0	0	0	0	0	0	0	0	0	0	—	—	0	0	0
Walter Beall		Did not play															
Garland Braxton		Did not play															
Herb McQuaid		Did not play															
team total		7	223	21	54	10	1	4	20	31	31	1	.242	.350	189	83	7

Double Plays-3
Left on Bases-55

REGULAR SEASON STATISTICS

		Main Pos	G	AB	R	H	2B	3B	HR	RBI	BB	SO	SB	BA	SA
Lou Gehrig		1b	155	572	135	179	47	20	16	107	105	72	6	.313	.549
Tony Lazzeri		2b	155	589	79	162	28	14	18	114	54	96	16	.275	.462
Mark Koenig		ss	147	617	93	167	26	8	5	62	43	37	4	.271	.363
Joe Dugan		3b	123	434	39	125	19	5	1	64	25	16	2	.288	.362
Babe Ruth		of	152	495	139	184	30	5	47	145	144	76	11	.372	.737
Earle Combs		of	145	606	113	181	31	12	8	56	47	23	8	.299	.429
Bob Meusel		of	108	413	73	130	22	3	12	81	37	32	16	.315	.470
Hank Severeid	c	c	41	127	13	34	8	1	0	13	13	4	1	.268	.346
Ben Paschal		of	96	258	46	74	12	3	7	33	26	35	7	.287	.438
Pat Collins		c	102	290	41	83	11	3	7	35	73	55	3	.286	.417
Mike Gazella		3b	66	168	21	39	6	0	0	21	25	24	2	.232	.268
Spence Adams		2b	28	25	7	3	1	0	0	1	3	7	1	.120	.160
Benny Bengough		c	36	84	9	32	6	0	0	14	7	4	1	.381	.452
Roy Carlyle	d	of	35	53	3	20	5	1	0	11	4	9	0	.377	.509
Aaron Ward		2b	22	31	5	10	2	0	0	3	2	6	0	.323	.387
Herb Pennock		p	40	85	8	18	2	0	0	6	10	8	0	.212	.235
Waite Hoyt		p	40	76	4	16	3	0	0	4	0	8	0	.211	.250
Dutch Ruether	e	p-ph	13	21	2	2	0	0	0	0	0	1	0	.095	.095
Bob Shawkey		p	29	35	4	9	1	0	0	3	3	6	0	.257	.286
Urban Shocker		p	41	76	6	13	1	0	0	4	10	20	0	.171	.184
Myles Thomas		p	33	43	1	5	0	0	0	1	1	7	0	.116	.116
Sad Sam Jones		p	44	49	3	10	1	0	0	4	3	16	1	.204	.224
Walter Beall		p	20	22	3	3	0	0	0	1	5	7	0	.136	.136
Garland Braxton		p	37	20	0	6	0	0	0	1	1	5	0	.300	.300
Herb McQuaid		p	17	7	0	0	0	0	0	0	0	1	0	.000	.000
team total			155	5221	847	1508	262	75	121	794	642	580	79	.289	.437

c-from Washington
d-from Boston (A)
e-from Washington
Honey Barnes (c), Nick Cullop (ph), Kiddo Davis (of), Fred Merkle (1b), Bill Skiff (c), Hank Johnson (p) also played for the Yankees during the season.

PITCHING

ST. LOUIS CARDINALS

WORLD SERIES STATISTICS

	G	GS	CG	IP	H	R	ER	BB	SO	W	L	SV	ERA
Pete Alexander	3	2	2	20⅓	12	4	3	4	17	2	0	1	1.33
Bill Sherdel	2	2	1	17	15	5	4	8	3	0	2	0	2.12
Jesse Haines	3	2	1	16⅔	13	2	2	9	5	2	0	0	1.08
Flint Rhem	1	1	0	4	7	3	3	2	4	0	0	0	6.75
Hi Bell	1	0	0	2	4	2	2	1	1	0	0	0	9.00
Wild Bill Hallahan	1	0	0	2	2	1	1	3	1	0	0	0	4.50
Vic Keen	1	0	0	1	0	0	0	0	0	0	0	0	0.00
Art Reinhart	1	0	0	0	1	4	4	4	0	0	1	0	∞
Syl Johnson	Did not play												
Allan Sothoron	Did not play												
Ed Clough	Did not play												
team total	7	7	4	63	54	21	19	31	31	4	3	1	2.71

REGULAR SEASON STATISTICS

		G	GS	CG	IP	H	ER	BB	SO	W	L	Pct	SV	ShO	ERA
Pete Alexander	b	23	16	11	148	136	48	24	35	9	7	.563	2	2	2.92
Bill Sherdel		34	29	17	235	255	91	49	59	16	12	.571	0	3	3.49
Jesse Haines		33	21	14	183	186	66	48	46	13	4	.765	1	3	3.25
Flint Rhem		34	34	20	258	241	92	75	72	20	7	.741	0	1	3.21
Hi Bell		27	7	3	85	82	30	17	27	6	6	.500	2	0	3.18
Wild Bill Hallahan		19	3	0	57	45	23	32	28	1	4	.200	0	0	3.63
Vic Keen		26	21	12	152	179	77	42	29	10	9	.526	0	1	4.56
Art Reinhart		27	11	9	143	159	67	47	26	10	5	.667	0	0	4.22
Syl Johnson		19	6	1	49	54	23	15	10	0	3	.000	1	0	4.22
Allan Sothoron		15	4	1	43	37	20	16	19	3	3	.500	0	0	4.19
Ed Clough		1	0	0	2	5	5	3	0	0	0	—	0	0	22.50
team total		156	156	90	1399	1423	570	397	365	89	65	.578	6	10	3.67

NEW YORK YANKEES

WORLD SERIES STATISTICS

	G	GS	CG	IP	H	R	ER	BB	SO	W	L	SV	ERA
Herb Pennock	3	2	2	22	13	3	3	4	8	2	0	0	1.23
Waite Hoyt	2	2	1	15	19	8	2	1	10	1	1	0	1.20
Bob Shawkey	3	1	0	10	8	7	6	2	7	0	1	0	5.40
Urban Shocker	2	1	0	7⅔	13	7	5	0	3	0	1	0	5.87
Dutch Ruether	1	1	0	4⅓	7	4	2	2	1	0	1	0	4.16
Myles Thomas	2	0	0	3	3	1	1	0	0	0	0	0	3.00
Sad Sam Jones	1	0	0	1	2	1	1	2	1	0	0	0	9.00
Walter Beall	Did not play												
Garland Braxton	Did not play												
Herb McQuaid	Did not play												
team total	7	7	3	63	65	31	20	11	30	3	4	0	2.86

REGULAR SEASON STATISTICS

		G	GS	CG	IP	H	ER	BB	SO	W	L	Pct	SV	ShO	ERA
Herb Pennock		40	33	19	266	294	107	43	78	23	11	.676	2	1	3.62
Waite Hoyt		40	27	12	218	224	93	62	79	16	12	.571	4	1	3.84
Bob Shawkey		29	10	3	104	102	42	37	63	8	7	.522	3	1	3.63
Urban Shocker		41	33	19	258	272	97	71	59	19	11	.633	2	0	3.38
Dutch Ruether	e	5	5	1	36	32	14	18	8	2	3	.400	0	0	3.50
Myles Thomas		33	13	3	140	140	66	65	38	6	6	.500	0	0	4.24
Sad Sam Jones		39	23	6	161	186	89	80	69	9	8	.529	5	1	4.98
Walter Beall		20	9	1	82	71	32	68	56	2	4	.333	1	0	3.51
Garland Braxton		37	1	0	67	71	20	19	30	5	1	.833	2	0	2.69
Herb McQuaid		17	1	0	38	48	26	13	6	1	0	1.000	0	0	6.16
team total		155	155	64	1372	1442	588	478	486	91	63	.591	20	4	3.86

Total Attendance—328,051 Average Attendance—46,864 Winning Player's Share—$5,585 Losing Player's Share—$3,418

1926

St. Louis Cardinals vs. New York Yankees

Babe Ruth. His very name brings back memories to the dwindling number of fans who saw this gargantuan figure on toothpick-thin legs boom parabolic shots into the stands time and again, and then mince his way around the bases with cat-like steps. To the typical adult, he is a legendary figure who gave color to his age, as John L. Sullivan gave color to an earlier age. To the younger generation, he is merely a name, spoken in reverential terms by their elders and used as a benchmark for modern ball players like Aaron and Maris.

But Babe Ruth was more than a name. He was an institution, a deity. One prominent Methodist minister even suggested, "If St. Paul were living today, he would know Babe Ruth's batting average." Legions of sportswriters followed his every move, forming a cult of followers with high priests like Runyon, Lardner, Rice and Broun spreading the Ruthian gospel. He was The Sultan of Swat, The Wizard of Whack, The King of Clout, The Behemoth of Biff and, of course, The Bambino.

Each day brought new accolades and exaggerated stories about the man who had become a legend in his own time. And with every move he made—real or imagined—chronicled in print, his legendary status became enhanced, so heavily laced with fiction and mawkish exaggeration that he became half-man, half-myth. The problem was, which half was myth?

The year 1925 was watershed year for Ruth. During his 11-year career, he had played on six pennant winners, three second-place teams, one third-place club and on only one second-division team, the 1919 Red Sox. Even then, he had won the home run and runs-batted-in championships and by the end of the season been traded to the Yankees in the biggest deal, up until that time, in baseball history. During his last seven years, playing as a full-time outfielder, he had averaged almost 40 homers, 120 RBIs, batted at a .357 clip and had a .740 slugging average. He was a superstar of the first magnitude.

But, at the age of 30, all that seemed to be behind him; for even if such a rare bird as Ruth could fly on one wing, he could not fly on none. And 1925 was the year when Ruth collapsed from some unexplainable malady in spring training, causing him to be borne back to New York on a stretcher for observation. The romantics called it "The Great Bellyache," ascribing his pains to a massive overdose of hot dogs and soda pop. Others, influenza. And some had the indelicacy to label it a social disease. But whatever it was, it laid the Babe low for the first few months of the '25 season.

When Ruth finally rejoined the team, he was not the robust Ruth of days of yore. And his prowess with the bat showed it. His once-healthy batting average hovered somewhere in the .240s and his home run production was equally anemic, by

Ruthian standards. The team suffered accordingly, falling to seventh place, its lowest perch since 1914, the year before they had been purchased by Colonel Jacob Ruppert.

But if Ruth's on-the-field pursuits were failing, his off-the-field ones were not. He kept his own counsel—refusing to heed the words of manager Miller Huggins—and kept his own company, usually four or five of the prettiest heads of bleached locks found in any one of the eight American League cities his travels took him to. (When Ruth's first roommate on the Yankees was asked whom he roomed with, he answered, "Babe Ruth's suitcase.")

To add to his—and the team's—problems, Ruth continually argued with Huggins, especially now that Huggins had lost all patience with his talented team, which was wallowing deep in the second division. Their constant bickering would take the form of Huggins wanting to know "how anybody expected the team to win anything when the players obviously didn't bother to keep in shape?" delivered in a sotto voce manner. Ruth knew who he was talking about and challenged him with criticisms of his running of the club. After a few barbed comments, the remainder of the discussion would descend into a name-calling contest, with Huggins challenging Ruth, "If you don't like the way I'm running the club, you can pack up and go home," and Ruth answering, "Why don't you send me home, you shrimp?" Huggins would throw another barb in Ruth's direction, sounding something like, "Go home, you big ape, if that's what you want," and Ruth would challenge him with, "Send me. You haven't got guts enough." That would usually conclude the festivities, except for Ruth's final gratuitous comment, as Hug walked out of the room: "Can you imagine that guy? Talking to *me* like that!"

As the team played worse and worse and Huggins's patience began to wear thinner and thinner, Ruth continued to stay out longer and longer. Something had to happen. That something came in St. Louis. The Babe had come back to the Hotel Buckingham hours after Huggins's 1 A.M. curfew and further compounded the felony by reporting to Sportsman's Park equally late that afternoon, missing batting practice. Huggins was waiting for him. "Sorry, Hug," said Ruth, blithely removing his jacket, "I had some business to attend to." In an expressionless voice the little manager said, "Don't bother to get into your uniform today." The Babe wheeled on him. "What did you say?" he demanded. "I said for you not to bother." Huggins now pulled himself up to his full 5'6½" height and said, "And I'll tell you something else, too . . . ." He gripped his belt, his voice shaking, "This is the finish. You're fined $5000 and suspended indefinitely."

The hulking 6'2", 220-pound raging Ruth now hovered over his manager. "You'll never get away with this, you little shit.

I'll never play another game of ball for you. I'll go to New York and see Jake [Ruppert]. You don't think he'll stand for this, do you? Why, he'll . . ." and he sputtered, too angry to get the words out. But Huggins, who had already cleared his decision with Ruppert, stood his ground and merely said, "Do as you please," and walked out of the clubhouse onto the field.

Ruth hurried to New York, writers in tow, to see the owner who, he was sure, would back up his star. But the one-man rebellion was doomed from the start. Ruppert backed Huggins, and Ruth went back to the ball club, his mood changed from apoplectic to apologetic. After reinstatement, the thoroughly chastised Ruth proceeded to raise his 1925 batting average from .246 to .290, and his home run total to 25, finishing third in the league and second on his own team, the first time that had ever happened to him—the second would be his last year as a Yankee. But it still was not a vintage Ruth year. He would have to do better, the press wrote, if the Yankees were to do better. He would, and they would.

As the greatest star in baseball, playing in the media capital of the world, Ruth received more attention and coverage in the press than any other athlete of the decade, if not the century. There may have been several other baseball stars worthy of press consideration and coverage, particularly in the National League, but they didn't seem to get the "ink" Ruth did. Their sin was not that they might be playing in the National League—which had two teams in New York—but that they were not playing for a New York team.

Among many, two who were continually overlooked were Rogers Hornsby, the National League's leading batter for the last six years, and Grover Cleveland Alexander, the National League's winningest pitcher. By the end of 1926, New York writers would have a chance to get a good look at these two superstars.

Rogers Hornsby broke into big league baseball as a 19-year-old shortstop in 1915. He not only didn't seem destined for baseball immortality, he hardly seemed destined for baseball longevity. In his first major league game he struck out the first two times he came up against the Reds' overpowering right-hander Fred Toney, and compounded his embarrassment by muffing his first fielding opportunity, dropping a perfect throw from catcher Frank Snyder on an attempted steal.

But Cardinal manager Miller Huggins—called "The Mighty Mite" because of his size and somewhat anemic-looking 140-pound frame—took the equally anemic-looking 135-pound freshman under his diminutive wing. First, he suggested that Hornsby change his batting stance; second, he ordered him to stop using the Fred Clarke model bat—named after the player-manager of the Pittsburgh Pirates—because he was too light to swing it from the end of the bat. "They throw a lot harder in the majors than Class D," Huggins told his young infielder, "and you don't have the strength to get the bat around. Try choking up on it."

Hornsby got his batting average up to .246 in 18 games that year, but that didn't seem to impress manager Huggins—whose sixth-place Cardinals led the National League in batting—and he was farmed out at the end of the year.

However, a now-heavier Hornsby made the club the following spring—as a third baseman. In one of his first games he came up against Grover Cleveland Alexander, who had won 31 games for the pennant-winning Phillies the previous year, and who would win 30 more in their little bandbox of a park

that year. With the Phillies far ahead, catcher Bill Killefer, who had played with Rogers's brother Everett in the Texas League, said, "Kid, here comes a good fastball. Let's see what you can do with it." What Hornsby did with it was hit it against the left-field fence for a double. Figuring that if he could hit the great Alexander like that, he should be able to hit anyone, a now-confident Hornsby raised his second-year average to .313, tops on the Cardinals and fourth-best in the National League. He was on his way.

By 1920, hitting the ball against Alexander as well as everyone else, Hornsby took his first batting crown with a .370 average. He was to follow that with successive championships in 1921, 1922, 1923, 1924 and 1925, a six-year span that saw him average .397, the highest six-year average in baseball history, and become the National League's superstar, one to rival Cobb and Ruth.

Hornsby was now regarded as the premier second baseman of the '20s, if not of all time, by most observers. One contemporary who did not agree with the consensus was Ty Cobb, who selected Eddie Collins on his all-time team. When Ted Williams asked him about it, he merely said, "Hornsby couldn't go backwards." But, argued Williams, "He had a higher batting average than you did one year." With that, Cobb never again spoke to Williams.

However, while Hornsby's batting average and stock were soaring, the rest of the Redbirds were still reminiscent of the Cardinals of old. In the first 24 years of the twentieth century the Cardinals had finished in the first division just five times, the same number of times they had finished last. The citizens of St. Louis had not had a winning team since the days of Chris Von der Ahe's "Vonderboys," four-time winners in the old American Association, 1885–89. They had lost patience with their teams and had resorted to the old-time doggerel once used to ridicule the Washington team (which was now the World Champion), chanting "First in shoes, first in booze, last in the National League."

After a sixth-place finish in 1924, the '25 Cardinals, under the leadership of manager Branch Rickey, seemed destined—like water—to find their own level again, and by Memorial Day were floundering with a 13–25 record. It was then that owner Sam Breadon decided to make a managerial change, kicking Rickey upstairs and naming his second baseman as player-manager. Hornsby, who set down strict rules for his fellow players, including not watching movies for fear it would harm their eyes, led by example, not words, leading the National League in hitting for the sixth straight year and winning his second triple crown in the process. He inspired his charges to play at a 64–51 pace and to finish in fourth place.

But even with Hornsby leading the team at bat and in the field, the St. Louis Cardinals hardly looked like the team to beat in '26. In fact, the team that Hornsby took to spring training was almost identical to the team he had inherited from Rickey on Memorial Day, 1925, with the single exception of shortstop Tommy Thevenow, whom Hornsby had recalled from Syracuse midway during the 1925 season. His pitching staff included knuckleballer Jesse "Pop" Haines, coming off a 13–14 season; and Flint Rhem, the reprobate pitcher—who had once come staggering back to the Cardinals after being AWOL for four days. Rhem claimed he had been kidnapped by gangsters, locked in a hotel room and forced to drink great quantities of liquor at the point of a gun, making Rickey admit, "You couldn't disprove his story by the way he smelled."

The pitching staff also included Allen Sothoron, who, five years after the passage of the rule prohibiting the use of "foreign substances on the ball," still threw the best emeryball in baseball; and little Willie Sherdell, the left-hander who had led the National League in pitching percentage in '25. Together, the Cardinals' "Big 4" had amassed a 46–43 record in 1925. Not the stuff dreams are made of.

The team afield was good, with potential signs of greatness, but nothing more. Outside of Hornsby at second, at first, Sunny Jim Bottomley, who two years before had set the all-time record for most RBIs in one game with 12, and Chick Hafey in right field, the remainder of the team was pedestrian: Thevenow at short, Lester Bell at third, and Ray Blades and Ralph Shinners in center. Behind the plate was Bob O'Farrell, picked up by Rickey in a trade with the Cubs just before he was relieved of his duties.

For six weeks the Cardinals looked like every Cardinal team of yore, unable to put it all together and mired in the second division. Then Hornsby put together a deal with the New York Giants, sending them Heinie Mueller for outfielder Billy Southworth, who took his place in the outfield with Hafey and young Taylor Douthit, giving them instant offense.

Still, by June 22, they were only in fourth place and in desperate need of pitching help. On that date they got it, claiming aging Grover Cleveland Alexander from the Chicago Cubs for the $4000 waiver price.

"The Great Alex" had been around for 15 years, winning 328 games—including eight 20-game seasons and three 30-game seasons. However, his reputation was not based on his pitching prowess alone, for Alexander was equally adept at the bottle. (Although Alexander, who suffered occasional epileptic attacks which were mistakenly described as drunken shakes, could hardly have been as drunk as he was often reported to have been; otherwise, he would never have been able to take the mound. One time, after reading a newspaper story about another of his supposed drunken bouts, he looked up and smirked, "Good God, I was never as drunk as this fellow had to be who wrote this here story!") It was felt by most that Alexander's greatness was behind him; that he was dissipated, drank too much, and because he had broken his ankle in spring training that year, that he was through as a big league pitcher at 39.

But it wasn't his dissipation, drunkenness or disability that finished him with the Cubs. It was what Cub manager Joe McCarthy viewed as his insubordination. On this occasion McCarthy was running down the strengths and weaknesses of the opposing batters on the Dodgers, telling Alexander how to pitch to each. When the name of Rabbit Maranville, the ancient shortstop who had only the previous year been with the Cubs, came up, McCarthy said, "We'll have to switch signs whenever he gets on second base. He's smart enough to remember our signals from last year." Alexander quipped, "Well, now, if we thought there was much chance of this guy gettin' on second base, we wouldn't have got rid of him, would we?"

By the time the Cubs had moved on to Philadelphia, Alexander's remark had earned him a place on the waiver list, tossed onto baseball's scrap heap like an antique without worth, there to be picked up by any team in inverse order to current position in the standings. And the Cardinals stood fifth in line by virtue of their being in fourth place on that magic day in June of 1926.

Hornsby, who had heard all of the stories about Alex—all of which intimated he carried a gin bottle more often than a glove—still wanted him for his team. He was supported by his coach Bill Killefer, the same Bill Killefer who had caught Alex for 11 years and knew that Alexander pitched better drunk that anyone else did sober. Together they went to Rickey, now the general manager, and asked him to claim Alexander on waivers. After the four teams below them in the standings passed on him, they got in Alexander the pitching help they needed. And the linchpin that was to make the Cardinals the World Champions.

Five days later Alexander pitched his first game for the Cards, facing his old team, the Chicago Cubs. Giving up only four hits, Alexander beat the Cubs 3–2 in ten innings, and after the game tipped his slightly askew hat when he passed Joe McCarthy on his way to the locker room.

With Alexander contributing nine victories, Rhem, 20, Sherdell, 16 and Haines, 13, the Cardinals went into the lead in early September. With one week to go, they had a one-game lead over the pursuing Cincinnati Reds.

It was at this moment that Hornsby, the manager, had his first run-in with Breadon, the owner. They had just lost a close game to third-place Pittsburgh when Breadon came into the clubhouse and demanded that they play three exhibition games that had been scheduled, but that Hornsby had attempted to have Breadon cancel. But Breadon wanted the revenue—pennant or no pennant—and stuck his head into the room to holler: "You're going to play those exhibitions, Hornsby, and that's final!"

Hornsby attempted to stand up for his players by hollering back, "Hell, that's all right with me. We get a total of three thousand dollars for three games and take the chance of getting some players hurt. But if you want to risk the half-million dollars we'd get for winning the pennant on those silly exhibition games, then I'm not going to play all my regulars."

But screaming match or no, the Cardinals played those three exhibition games against Syracuse, Hartford and New Haven, winning all three and losing leftfielder Chick Hafey in the process. Hafey's injury almost cost them the pennant. But finally, on September 28, while Cincinnati was losing, they won a double-header in New York, to clinch St. Louis's first pennant.

Over in the American League, the pennant chase lasted one more day, with the New York Yankees, once ahead of the pack by a comfortable margin, barely edging out the fast-closing Cleveland Indians by three games. The Yankees, with Babe Ruth leading the league in home runs and RBIs, and finishing second in batting with a .372 average, were, like the Yankee teams of 1921–23, the best team money could buy. This time around they had built the best team by adding Earle Combs in center, Lou Gehrig at first, Tony Lazzeri at second and Mark Koenig at short. And, like most Yankee teams, they were favored to add the World Series to their already-won pennant.

The 1926 World Series was mammoth in every sense. It had the greatest attendance and receipts of any Series up to that time, the greatest stars performing and the greatest moment in all of Series history. The 1926 Series will be remembered by most as the one in which Grover Cleveland Alexander struck out Tony Lazzeri with the bases loaded in the seventh and last game to preserve a St. Louis victory. Ironically, most of those who recall it—either from experience or memory—recall it incorrectly, placing that moment, preserved in Series history like a rose pressed in pages of a scrapbook, as happening in the ninth inning of the final game. And almost no one remembers that it also was the Series in which Ruth hit three homers in one game, or that Alexander won his two starts or that the Series ended in a strange and bizarre play. Just that Alexander struck out Lazzeri.

With Yankee ace left-hander Herb Pennock pitching three-hit ball, the Yankees won the opening game, played in New York's huge Yankee Stadium, 3–2, over Wee Willie Sherdell, with "Pop" Haines in relief. The second game went to the Cardinals, 6–2, as Grover Cleveland Alexander set down the last 21 Yankees after a third-inning single by Earle Combs. Game three, back at Sportsman's Park in St. Louis, saw the Cards take the Series lead, two games to one, on "Pop" Haines's five-hitter.

Yankee bats, quiescent during the first three games, exploded in game four, as New York, led by Babe Ruth's three massive homers, blasted 14 hits off Flint Rhem and four other pitchers, to win 10–5 and even up the Series. Game five was a rematch of the first game, with Pennock and Sherdell each pitching their best ball, Pennock giving up just one run. The Yankees grouped three hits in the top of the ninth to tie the game and send it into extra innings, and won it in the tenth, 3–2, to take a 3–2 lead in games back to Yankee Stadium.

Alexander went to the mound for game six and won with an eight-hitter, although he never had to extend himself, as the Cardinals raked three Yankee pitchers for thirteen hits and a 10–2 win. All of this was to serve as table setting for game seven, one of the most famous in World Series history.

The game, played in the cold and dreary autumnal weather of New York, saw Jesse Haines, winner of the third game, go against Waite Hoyt, winner of game four. In the third inning, pitching carefully to Ruth, whom he had walked in the first, Haines tossed a tantalizing inside knuckleball. Timing his swing perfectly, Ruth provided all of the momentum as the ball took flight and cleared the bleacher fence, deep in right center, passing directly over the words "World's Champions" in the Gem razor ad. That should have been enough to insure Hoyt and the Yankees the game.

However, fate, which had decided every Series that had gone the seven-game limit, once again determined the winner, dealing the cards to St. Louis in the form of breaks, just as breaks had decided the last games of three previous seven-game Series—in the '24 Series, McNeeley's grounder hit a pebble and bounded over Lindstrom's head; in the '12 Series, Snodgrass dropped Engle's fly; and in the '25 Series, Peckinpaugh again allowed the winning run to score on an error. This time fate was to point her capricious finger at two men named Koenig and Meusel.

It came in the fourth inning. After Hornsby led off the top of the inning by meekly grounding out to Hoyt, Bottomley singled to right. Then Hoyt got Bell to drill a one-hop grounder straight at Koenig, a sure double play. But Koenig, in his haste to shovel the ball over to Lazzeri, never got the handle, and bobbled it, putting runners on first and second with one out. Fate, however, wasn't through with Hoyt. For the next batter up, Hafey, with a count of two strikes and no balls, barely managed to poke a weak fly out into left field, which fell between the two marked men, Koenig and Meusel, to load the bases. Bob O'Farrell, next up, hit a high fly to left center.

Meusel, having a stronger arm than centerfielder Combs, waved Combs off the ball so he could make the throw to the plate in an attempt to catch the slow Bottomley. But even as he positioned himself under the ball, fate was still toying with the Yankees, and somehow caused the ball to pop into his glove—and out again. Bottomley scored and the bases remained loaded. The next batter up, Tommy Thevenow—who had the lowest regular-season batting average among all of the starters on both teams, and the highest in the Series, .417—proved that fate was still on the Cardinals' side by catching one of Hoyt's fastballs with the end of his bat and looping a hit into right field, scoring two more unearned runs.

The Yankees got one run back in the bottom of the sixth, and came into the bottom of the seventh trailing 3–2. Combs opened the inning with a single and went to second on Koenig's sacrifice. Ruth was intentionally walked, his third pass of the game, to put runners on first and second with only one out. Meusel, with an opportunity to redeem himself, hit one of Haines's knucklers into a force play, leaving runners on first and third, two out. Gehrig was now up. His bat had won one game with a single and his double helped to win another. After getting two quick strikes on him, Haines seemed to falter, and the next four pitches were balls, loading the bases.

Haines turned around to Hornsby and wiggled his hand, a cross between "Come here" and "Something's wrong." What was wrong was that he had worn the skin off the index finger of his right hand throwing his knuckler, and was asking to be taken out of the game. Hornsby, who had left-hander Sherdell warming up in the bullpen, wanted a right-hander to pitch to the next man up, Tony Lazzeri. Lazzeri, although only a rookie, had a reputation for power, having hit 60 homers and batted in 222 runs at Salt Lake City the year before. Hornsby wanted a right-hander; and the best he had was Alexander.

So he yelled "Alexander," and after a momentary delay a figure emerged from the left-field bullpen, hat at a rakish angle and slouched over, ambling toward the mound, but in no apparent hurry to get there. It was Grover Cleveland Alexander, coming in after pitching a complete game the day before—and as legend would have it, celebrating all evening. Hornsby was to recall later, "Alexander could have been drunk for all I cared. Hell, I'd rather have him pitch a crucial game for me drunk than anyone I've ever known sober."

The confrontation was set: Alexander versus Lazzeri. The inning, the game and the Series hung in the balance.

Hornsby trotted halfway out into the outfield to meet his reliever. "Well, the bases are full, Lazzeri's up and there ain't no place to put him," the manager told his pitcher as Alexander handed the mascot his sweater. "Well, guess I'll have to take care of him, then," answered the unflappable Alex, moving inexorably towards the mound, Hornsby at his side.

After only three warm-up pitches, Alexander was ready to go. He adjusted his cap, not quite bringing it back to the front of his head, fooled around with his belt and then turned to make sure that all of his teammates were ready. The man who had once thrown only 76 pitches while winning a nine-inning game, and who pitched fast because he didn't want to "let those sons of bitches stand up there and think on my time," was now ready.

His first pitch was low for a ball. He took the throw from O'Farrell and returned it, almost immediately. This one caught the corner for a strike. One and one. His next pitch was outside and Lazzeri caught it on the meat part of the bat. It looked like a home run all the way. The Yankees all emerged from the dugout, standing on the steps to greet Lazzeri when he crossed the plate. Then, just before it went into the left-field stands, the ball curved, going foul by no more than ten inches. Fate had again frowned on the Yankees. Alex, disdaining any more outside fastballs, threw Lazzeri a low curveball which one writer described as something "the Singer midgets couldn't have hit." Lazzeri swung and missed. The confrontation and inning were over. And, although it was only the end of the seventh inning, the Series was also over.

In the eighth, Alexander retired the Yankees on a grounder, a foul fly and a pop-up, one—two—three. All that stood between him and a masterful save were Combs, Koenig and Ruth, the three batters he would face in the bottom of the ninth.

Combs and Koenig both grounded out, Bell to Bottomley. Now he faced Babe Ruth, who had single-handedly beaten the Cards in game four and had almost won the final game before fate stepped in. Pitching carefully, Alex ran the count to 3–2 on Ruth. Then, the man who could throw a ball through a gallon tomato can from the pitcher's mound for fifteen minutes straight without missing, threw a curve ball on the outside corner of the plate and started to walk off the mound. But plate umpire George Hildebrand called it "Ball four" and Ruth had his eleventh walk of the Series, his fourth of the game.

Alexander wheeled around to Hildebrand. "What's wrong with that pitch?" he demanded. Hildebrand answered, "Missed by this much, Alex," holding out his hands to show no more than two inches. "For that much," Alex answered, ambling back to the mound, "you might have given an old son of a gun like me a break."

But the breaks were still with the Cardinals. And with Bob Meusel up at bat, Alex delivered a curve exactly where the last one to Ruth had been. This time Hildebrand signaled "Strike." It was to be the last pitch of the Series.

For at that moment some strange spirit moved Ruth, who was the co-holder of the Series record for most stolen bases in one inning, to take off for second. Asked years later what had possessed him to run, he had answered, "Nobody told me. I just decided to go. So I went." If his move was calculated to be a surprise, it came as none to catcher O'Farrell, who rifled the ball down to Hornsby at second. Hornsby merely held his glove out to catch the throw and Ruth lumbered into it for the last out of the Series. Ruth jumped up to shake Hornsby's ungloved hand.

The Cardinals were World Champions and Hornsby and Alexander were the toasts of St. Louis—and the nation. By the beginning of the next year, Hornsby was gone from St. Louis, a result of his failure to get along with Breadon. But that's another story. For the moment—he *was* St. Louis.

Official Souvenir Program
World Series 1926

Major League Advisory Council

Hon. KENESAW M. LANDIS
Commissioner

© Moffitt,
Chicago

B. B. JOHNSON
President American League

JOHN A. HEYDLER
President National League

Mr.Joseph Kaufman, President,
American Safety Razor Corporation,
Johnson & Jay Streets,
Brooklyn,New York.

My dear Mr.Kaufman:

      Thanks for your congratulations. That
Gem Razor sure is the world s champion of the "shave
league", as you so aptly say on the big sign at the
Stadium.

      The boys had many a close shave this season,
but the Gem gave them one every day.

              Very truly yours,

              Miller J.Huggins

JACOB RUPPERT
President
American League Baseball Club of N. Y.

EDWARD G. BARROW
Secretary
American League Baseball Club of N. Y.

Keep costly upkeep out of your home

If you are going to build, buy or remodel a home you will find these books helpful.

Sent without charge
Write for them

COPPER & BRASS
RESEARCH ASSOCIATION
25 Broadway, New York

BRANCH RICKEY
Vice-President
St. Louis National League Baseball Club

SAM. BREADON
President
St. Louis National League Baseball Club

17. Thomas, p.	20. McQuaid, p.	23. Adams, i. f.	26. Paschal, o. f.	**Coaches** Chas. O'Leary Fred. Merkle	**Manager** Miller Huggins
18. Braxton, p.	21. Bengough, c.	24. Ward, i. f.			
19. Beall, p.	22. Gazella, i. f.	25. Carlyle, o. f.			

NEW YORK		1	2	3	4	5	6	7	8	9	10	AB	R	1B	SH	P.O	A	E
1. Combs	c. f.																	
2. Koenig	s. s.																	
3. Ruth	r. f.																	
4. Meusel	l. f.																	
5. Gehrig	1 b.																	
6. Lazzeri	2 b.																	
7. Dugan	3 b.																	
8. Severeid / 9. Collins	c.																	
10 Pennock 11 Ruether 12 Shocker 14 Hoyt 15 Jones 16 Shawkey	p.																	

UMPIRES
T. H. Connally
George Hildebrand

Earned Runs.....Two-Base Hits.....Three-Base Hits.....Home Runs....Passed Balls....Wild Pitches....

Bases on Balls....Bases on Hit by Pitched Ball....Struck Out....Left on Bases....Double Plays....Time...

	15. Keen, p.	18. Sothoron, p.	21. Johnson, p.	24. Toporcer, i. f.	**Coaches**
	16. Reinhart, p.	19. Clough, p.	22. Warwick, c.	25. Holm, o. f.	William Killefer, Jr.
	17. H. Bell, p.	20. Hallahan, p.	23. Flowers, i. f.	26. Blades, o. f.	Otto Williams

ST. LOUIS

		1	2	3	4	5	6	7	8	9	10	AB	R	1B	SH	P.O	A	E
1. Douthit	c. f.																	
2. Southworth	r. f.																	
3. Hornsby	s. b.																	
4. Bottomley	f. b.																	
5. L. Bell	3 b.																	
6. Hafey	l. f.																	
7. O'Farrell / 8. Vick	c.																	
9. Thevenow	s. s.																	
10. Haines / 11. Sherdel / 12. Alexander / 14. Rhem	p.																	

UMPIRES
Henry O'Day
William Klem

Earned Runs....Two-Base Hits....Three-Base Hits....Home Runs....Passed Balls....Wild Pitches....
Bases on Balls....Bases on Hit by Pitched Ball....Struck Out....Left on Bases....Double Plays....Time...

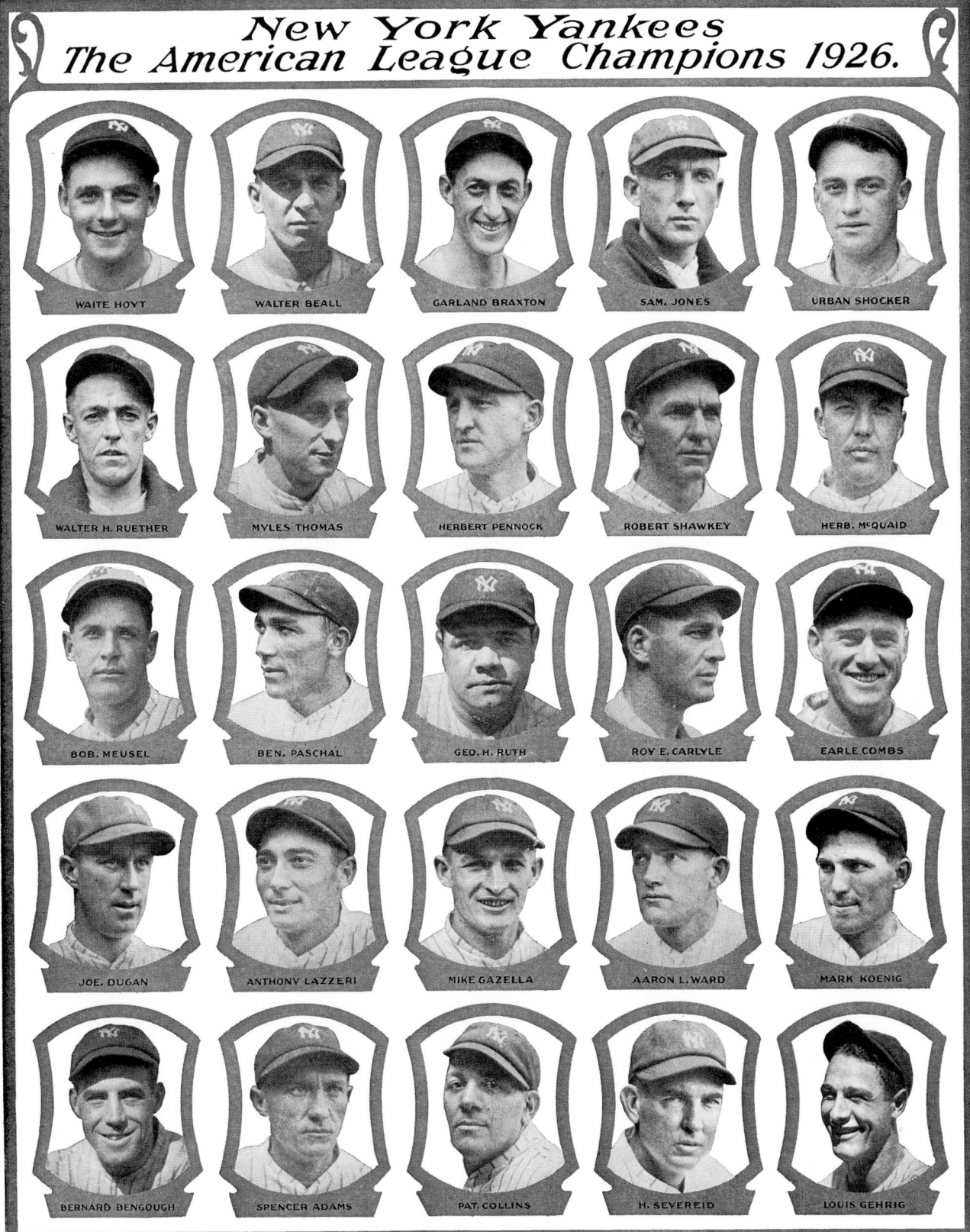

New York Yankees
The American League Champions 1926.

WAITE HOYT · WALTER BEALL · GARLAND BRAXTON · SAM. JONES · URBAN SHOCKER

WALTER H. RUETHER · MYLES THOMAS · HERBERT PENNOCK · ROBERT SHAWKEY · HERB. McQUAID

BOB. MEUSEL · BEN. PASCHAL · GEO. H. RUTH · ROY E. CARLYLE · EARLE COMBS

JOE. DUGAN · ANTHONY LAZZERI · MIKE GAZELLA · AARON L. WARD · MARK KOENIG

BERNARD BENGOUGH · SPENCER ADAMS · PAT. COLLINS · H. SEVEREID · LOUIS GEHRIG

BENJAMIN BLOCK
PETER J. MALONEY
J HORACE BLOCK
WILLIAM B. ANDERSON
ALFRED L. ROSENER

PETER J. MALONEY, JR.
MAYER L. HALFF
ALBERT F. STRAIGHT
FRANK O. GRATTAN
WILLIAM B. GILES

Block, Maloney & Co.

Members of

New York Stock Exchange
New York Cotton Exchange
New York Coffee and Sugar Exchange
New York Produce Exchange

Chicago Board of Trade
Chicago Stock Exchange

74 BROADWAY
NEW YORK

Telephone — Hanover 9000

Branch Offices:

550 7th AVENUE
NEW YORK, N. Y.
Tel. Penn. 7907

RITZ CARLTON HOTEL
ATLANTIC CITY, N. J.

St. Louis Cardinals
The National League Champions 1926.

JESSE J. HAINES — SYLVESTER JOHNSON — CHARLES J. HAFEY — ARTHUR C. REINHART — HENRY A. VICK

D'ARCY R. FLOWERS — CHARLES F. RHEM — WILLIAM A. HALLAHAN — ALLAN S. SOTHORON — JAMES L. BOTTOMLEY

EDGAR GEO. CLOUGH — HOWARD V. KEEN — ROGERS HORNSBY — FRANCIS R. BLADES — ROSCOE A. HOLM

WILLIAM SOUTHWORTH — GROVER C. ALEXANDER — TAYLOR L. DOUTHIT — LESTER R. BELL — ROBERT A. O'FARRELL

THOS. J. THEVENOW — GEORGE TOPORCER — HERMAN S. BELL — FIRMAN N. WARWICK — WILLIAM H. SHERDEL

THE CORN EXCHANGE BANK
NEW YORK

Statement ~ September 17th, 1926

The Bank Owes to Depositors...................... $252,101,755.46

For this Purpose We Have:

Cash.. 40,049,398.75

Checks on Other Banks........................... 31,108,627.25

U. S. Government Securities...................... 55,504,798.43

Loans to Individuals and Corporations............ 30,055,716.82

Bonds.. 44,588,850.51

Loans.. 52,951,336.80

Bonds and Mortgages............................ 14,963,358.76

Banking Houses................................. 7,441,450.16

Total to Meet Indebtedness...................... $276,663,537.48

This Leaves a Capital and Surplus of............. $24,561,782. 02

Because it's toasted, the
hidden flavors of the world's
finest tobaccos are developed

LUCKY STRIKE

"IT'S TOASTED"

1934

St. Louis Cardinals
vs.
Detroit Tigers

1934 WORLD SERIES COMPOSITE BOX

	Wins	Composite Line Score												
St. Louis Cardinals (N.L.)	4	2	5	10	2	5	6	4	0	0	0	0	0	– 34
Detroit Tigers (A.L.)	3	0	1	5	2	0	5	1	6	2	0	0	1	– 23

Manager	Regular Season W	L	Pct.	G. Ahead
Frankie Frisch	95	58	.621	2
Mickey Cochrane	101	53	.656	7

BATTING AND FIELDING

ST. LOUIS CARDINALS

WORLD SERIES STATISTICS	Pos	G	AB	R	H	2B	3B	HR	RBI	BB	SO	SB	BA	SA	PO	A	E
Ripper Collins	1b	7	30	4	**11**	1	0	0	3	1	2	0	.367	.400	56	6	1
Frankie Frisch	2b	7	**31**	2	6	1	0	0	4	0	1	0	.194	.226	17	**27**	2
Leo Durocher	ss	7	27	4	7	1	**1**	0	0	0	0	0	.259	.370	13	17	0
Pepper Martin	3b	7	**31**	**8**	**11**	3	**1**	0	4	3	3	**2**	.355	.516	6	9	**3**
Jack Rothrock	rf	7	30	3	7	3	**1**	0	6	1	2	0	.233	.400	19	0	1
Ernie Orsatti	cf-ph	7	22	3	7	0	**1**	0	2	3	1	0	.318	.409	16	1	2
Joe Medwick	lf	7	29	4	**11**	0	**1**	**1**	5	1	7	0	**.379**	.552	9	0	0
Bill DeLancey	c	7	29	3	5	3	0	**1**	4	2	8	0	.172	.379	50	6	2
Chick Fullis	cf-lf	3	5	0	2	0	0	0	0	0	0	0	.400	.400	6	0	1
Spud Davis	ph	2	2	0	2	0	0	0	1	0	0	0	1.000	1.000			
Pat Crawford	ph	2	2	0	0	0	0	0	0	0	0	0	.000	.000			
Burgess Whitehead	pr-ss	1	0	0	0	0	0	0	0	0	0	0	—	—	1	0	0
Francis Healy		Did not play															
Dizzy Dean	p-pr	4	12	3	3	2	0	0	1	0	3	0	.250	.417	2	2	0
Paul Dean	p	2	6	0	1	0	0	0	2	0	1	0	.167	.167	0	0	1
Wild Bill Hallahan	p	1	3	0	0	0	0	0	0	0	1	0	.000	.000	1	3	1
Bill Walker	p	2	2	0	0	0	0	0	0	0	2	0	.000	.000	0	1	1
Tex Carleton	p	2	1	0	0	0	0	0	0	0	0	0	.000	.000	0	0	0
Dazzy Vance	p	1	0	0	0	0	0	0	0	0	0	0	—	—	0	0	0
Jim Mooney	p	1	0	0	0	0	0	0	0	0	0	0	—	—	0	1	0
Jesse Haines	p	1	0	0	0	0	0	0	0	0	0	0	—	—	0	0	0
team total		7	262	34	73	14	5	2	32	11	31	2	.279	.393	196	73	15

Double Plays—2
Left on Bases—49

REGULAR SEASON STATISTICS		Main Pos	G	AB	R	H	2B	3B	HR	RBI	BB	SO	SB	BA	SA
Ripper Collins		1b	154	600	116	200	40	12	**35**	128	57	50	2	.333	**.615**
Frankie Frisch		2b	140	550	74	168	30	6	3	75	45	10	11	.305	.398
Leo Durocher		ss	146	500	62	130	26	5	3	70	33	40	2	.260	.350
Pepper Martin		3b	110	454	76	131	25	11	5	49	32	41	23	.289	.425
Jack Rothrock		of	154	**647**	106	184	35	3	11	72	49	56	10	.284	.399
Ernie Orsatti		of	105	337	39	101	14	4	0	31	27	31	6	.300	.365
Joe Medwick		of	149	620	110	198	40	**18**	18	106	21	83	3	.319	.529
Bill DeLancey		c	93	253	41	80	18	3	13	40	41	37	1	.316	.565
Chick Fullis	a	of	69	199	21	52	9	1	0	26	14	11	4	.261	.317
Spud Davis		c	107	347	45	104	22	4	9	65	34	27	0	.300	.464
Pat Crawford		3b	61	70	3	19	2	0	0	16	5	3	0	.271	.300
Burgess Whitehead		2b-ss-3b	100	332	55	92	13	5	1	24	12	19	5	.277	.355
Francis Healy		c	15	13	1	4	1	0	0	1	0	2	0	.308	.385
Dizzy Dean		p	51	118	15	29	3	1	2	9	1	15	1	.246	.339
Paul Dean		p	39	83	6	20	4	0	0	3	1	12	0	.241	.289
Wild Bill Hallahan		p	32	55	3	10	1	0	0	6	2	16	0	.182	.200
Bill Walker		p	24	54	2	5	1	0	0	1	1	26	0	.093	.111
Tex Carleton		p	41	88	7	17	2	1	1	10	5	27	0	.193	.273
Dazzy Vance	b	p	19	15	1	2	0	0	1	1	0	6	0	.133	.333
Jim Mooney		p	32	19	0	1	0	0	0	2	0	1	0	.053	.053
Jesse Haines		p	37	19	1	3	0	0	0	0	1	5	0	.158	.158
team total			154	**5502**	**799**	**1582**	**294**	75	104	**748**	392	535	**69**	**.288**	**.425**

a—from Philadelphia (N)
b—from Cincinnati
Kiddo Davis (of), Buster Mills (of), Gene Moore (of), Lew Riggs (ph), Red Worthington (ph), Burleigh Grimes (p), Clarence Heise (p), Jim Lindsey (p), Flint Rhem (p), Jim Winford (p) also played for the Cardinals during the season.

DETROIT TIGERS

WORLD SERIES STATISTICS	Pos	G	AB	R	H	2B	3B	HR	RBI	BB	SO	SB	BA	SA	PO	A	E
Hank Greenberg	1b	7	28	4	9	2	**1**	**1**	**7**	4	**9**	1	.321	**.571**	**60**	4	1
Charlie Gehringer	2b	7	29	5	**11**	1	0	**1**	2	3	0	1	**.379**	.517	19	24	**3**
Billy Rogell	ss	7	29	3	8	1	0	0	4	1	4	1	.276	.310	11	18	**3**
Marv Owen	3b	7	29	0	2	0	0	0	1	0	5	1	.069	.069	9	9	2
Pete Fox	rf	7	28	1	8	**6**	0	0	2	1	4	0	.286	.500	15	0	0
Jo-Jo White	cf	7	23	6	3	0	0	0	0	**8**	4	1	.130	.130	22	0	1
Goose Goslin	lf	7	29	2	7	1	0	0	2	3	1	0	.241	.276	20	1	2
Mickey Cochrane	c	7	28	2	6	1	0	0	1	4	3	0	.214	.250	36	5	0
Gee Walker	ph	3	3	0	1	0	0	0	1	0	1	0	.333	.333			
Frank Doljack	ph-cf	2	2	0	0	0	0	0	0	0	0	0	.000	.000	1	0	0
Ray Hayworth	c	1	0	0	0	0	0	0	0	0	0	0	—	—	1	0	0
Flea Clifton		Did not play															
Heinie Schuble		Did not play															
Schoolboy Rowe	p	3	7	0	0	0	0	0	0	0	5	0	.000	.000	1	1	0
Tommy Bridges	p	3	7	0	1	0	0	0	0	1	4	0	.143	.143	0	2	0
Eldon Auker	p	2	4	0	0	0	0	0	0	0	2	0	.000	.000	0	2	0
Chief Hogsett	p	3	3	0	0	0	0	0	0	0	1	0	.000	.000	0	2	0
General Crowder	p	2	1	0	0	0	0	0	0	0	0	0	.000	.000	0	0	0
Firpo Marberry	p	2	0	0	0	0	0	0	0	0	0	0	—	—	0	1	0
Vic Sorrell		Did not play															
Carl Fischer		Did not play															
Luke Hamlin		Did not play															
team total		7	250	23	56	12	1	2	20	25	43	5	.224	.304	195	69	12

Double Plays—6
Left on Bases—64

REGULAR SEASON STATISTICS		Main Pos	G	AB	R	H	2B	3B	HR	RBI	BB	SO	SB	BA	SA
Hank Greenberg		1b	153	593	118	201	**63**	7	26	139	63	93	9	.339	.600
Charlie Gehringer		2b	154	601	**134**	**214**	50	7	11	127	99	25	11	.356	.517
Billy Rogell		ss	154	592	114	175	32	8	3	100	74	36	13	.296	.392
Marv Owen		3b	154	565	79	179	34	9	8	96	59	37	3	.317	.451
Pete Fox		of	128	516	101	147	31	2	2	45	49	53	25	.285	.364
Jo-Jo White		of	115	384	97	120	18	5	0	44	69	39	28	.313	.385
Goose Goslin		of	151	614	106	187	38	7	13	100	65	38	5	.305	.453
Mickey Cochrane		c	129	437	74	140	32	1	2	76	78	26	8	.320	.412
Gee Walker		of	98	347	54	104	19	2	6	39	19	20	20	.300	.418
Frank Doljack		of	56	120	15	28	7	1	1	19	13	15	2	.233	.333
Ray Hayworth		c	54	167	20	49	5	2	0	27	16	22	0	.293	.347
Flea Clifton		3b	24	16	3	1	0	0	0	1	1	2	0	.063	.063
Heinie Schuble		ss-3b	27	15	2	4	2	0	0	2	1	4	0	.267	.400
Schoolboy Rowe		p	51	109	15	33	8	1	2	22	6	20	0	.303	.450
Tommy Bridges		p	36	98	7	12	2	0	0	10	7	25	0	.122	.143
Eldon Auker		p	43	74	3	11	2	0	0	8	4	28	0	.149	.176
Chief Hogsett		p	26	13	0	3	0	0	0	1	0	5	0	.231	.231
General Crowder	c	p	9	30	1	4	0	0	0	0	0	4	0	.133	.133
Firpo Marberry		p	38	55	7	12	4	0	0	9	4	4	0	.218	.291
Vic Sorrell		p	28	37	1	4	0	0	0	0	5	9	0	.108	.108
Carl Fischer		p	20	31	1	2	0	0	0	3	1	6	0	.065	.065
Luke Hamlin		p	20	26	1	6	0	0	0	2	0	8	0	.231	.231
team total			154	**5475**	**958**	**1644**	**349**	53	74	**872**	639	528	**124**	**.300**	.424

c—from Washington
Cy Perkins (ph), Frank Reiber (ph), Icehouse Wilson (ph), Rudy York (c), Vic Frasier (p), Steve Larkin (p), Red Phillips (p) also played for the Tigers during the season.

PITCHING

ST. LOUIS CARDINALS

WORLD SERIES STATISTICS	G	GS	CG	IP	H	R	ER	BB	SO	W	L	SV	ERA
Dizzy Dean	**3**	**3**	**2**	**26**	20	6	5	5	**17**	**2**	1	0	1.73
Paul Dean	2	2	**2**	18	15	4	2	**7**	11	**2**	0	0	**1.00**
Wild Bill Hallahan	1	1	0	8⅓	6	2	2	4	6	0	0	0	2.16
Bill Walker	2	0	0	6⅓	6	7	5	6	2	0	**2**	0	7.11
Tex Carleton	2	1	0	3⅔	5	3	3	2	2	0	0	0	7.36
Dazzy Vance	1	0	0	1⅓	2	1	0	1	3	0	0	0	0.00
Jim Mooney	1	0	0	1	1	0	0	0	0	0	0	0	0.00
Jesse Haines	1	0	0	⅔	1	0	0	0	2	0	0	0	0.00
team total	7	7	4	65⅓	56	23	17	25	43	4	3	0	2.34

REGULAR SEASON STATISTICS		G	GS	CG	IP	H	ER	BB	SO	W	L	Pct	SV	ShO	ERA
Dizzy Dean		50	33	24	312	288	92	75	**195**	**30**	7	**.811**	7	7	2.65
Paul Dean		39	26	16	233	225	89	52	150	19	11	.633	2	5	3.44
Wild Bill Hallahan		32	26	10	163	195	77	66	70	8	12	.400	0	2	4.25
Bill Walker		24	19	10	153	160	53	66	76	12	4	.750	0	1	3.12
Tex Carleton		40	31	16	241	260	114	52	103	16	11	.593	2	0	4.26
Dazzy Vance	b	19	4	1	59	62	24	14	33	1	1	.500	1	0	3.66
Jim Mooney		32	7	1	82	114	50	49	27	2	4	.333	1	0	5.49
Jesse Haines		37	6	0	90	86	35	19	17	4	4	.500	1	0	3.50
team total		154	154	**78**	**1387**	1463	568	411	**689**	**95**	58	**.621**	16	**15**	3.69

DETROIT TIGERS

WORLD SERIES STATISTICS	G	GS	CG	IP	H	R	ER	BB	SO	W	L	SV	ERA
Schoolboy Rowe	**3**	2	**2**	21⅓	19	8	**7**	0	12	1	1	0	2.95
Tommy Bridges	**3**	2	1	17⅓	**21**	**9**	**7**	1	12	1	1	0	3.63
Eldon Auker	2	2	1	11⅓	16	8	**7**	5	2	1	1	0	5.56
Chief Hogsett	**3**	0	0	7⅓	6	1	1	3	3	0	0	0	1.23
General Crowder	2	1	0	6	6	4	1	1	2	0	1	0	1.50
Firpo Marberry	2	0	0	1⅔	5	4	4	1	0	0	0	0	21.60
Vic Sorrell	Did not play												
Carl Fischer	Did not play												
Luke Hamlin	Did not play												
team total	7	7	4	65	73	34	27	11	31	3	4	0	3.74

REGULAR SEASON STATISTICS		G	GS	CG	IP	H	ER	BB	SO	W	L	Pct	SV	ShO	ERA
Schoolboy Rowe		45	30	20	266	259	102	81	149	24	8	.750	1	3	3.45
Tommy Bridges		36	**35**	23	275	249	112	104	151	22	11	.667	1	3	3.67
Eldon Auker		43	18	10	205	234	78	56	86	15	7	.682	1	2	3.42
Chief Hogsett		26	0	0	50	61	24	19	23	3	2	.600	3	0	4.32
General Crowder	c	9	9	3	67	81	31	20	30	5	1	.833	0	1	4.16
Firpo Marberry		38	19	6	156	174	79	48	64	15	5	.750	3	1	4.56
Vic Sorrell		28	19	6	130	146	69	45	46	6	9	.400	2	0	4.78
Carl Fischer		20	15	4	95	107	46	38	39	6	4	.600	1	1	4.36
Luke Hamlin		20	5	1	75	87	45	44	30	2	3	.400	1	0	5.40
team total		154	154	74	1370	1467	618	488	640	**101**	53	**.656**	14	11	4.06

Total Attendance—281,510 Average Attendance—40,216 Winning Player's Share—$5,390 Losing Player's Share—$3,355

1934

St. Louis Cardinals vs. Detroit Tigers

On October 24, 1929, the stock market fell with a resounding Crash! The feverish twenties had exploded, to be replaced by the troubled thirties; and the word "unemployed," once a seldom-used adjective, now become an oft-used and ominous noun as every fourth worker would lose his job. The American Dream had become a nightmare. As it did, bread lines and bonus armies took the place of the boom and bust atmosphere of the 1920s. And people who couldn't fill their bellies with food looked for heroes to fill their souls with hope.

Baseball, which had given them Babe Ruth in the Era of Excess, would now provide them with two authentic tintypes—"Pepper" Martin and "Dizzy" Dean. Together, these two would comfort Americans, providing a tonic for their sagging spirit and allowing them to live vicariously through their heroes' daring exploits.

It was no coincidence that the hero of the World Series of 1931—the bleakest year in our economic history—would be a dirty-faced, underpaid, hungry-looking outfielder from the Oklahoma Osages, who had entered baseball on the rods of a freight train. Almost single-handedly, "Pepper" Martin had figuratively and literally stolen the '31 Series from the heavily favored A's, with his headfirst belly slides, made in heedless disregard of his personal safety (and made all the more daring by the fact that his slides were made without benefit of an athletic supporter). "All" Martin did in the first five games of the Series was to go 12 for 13, steal five bases, drive in five runs and score five more, accounting for all but one of the runs in the Cardinals' victories in games two and five. His exciting style of play gave the common man confidence that those at the bottom of the heap were sure to have their day.

But Martin was merely one part of the glamour team of the '30s, the St. Louis Cardinals. By 1934 the Cards had become known by their nickname, "The Gashouse Gang"—the result of a remark made by shortstop Leo Durocher who, having been asked by New York *Sun* columnist Frank Graham if the Cardinals were good enough to play in the American League, had answered, "They wouldn't let us play in the American League. They'd say we were just a lot of gashouse players"—and sported some of the most fanciful nicknames this side of the Seven Dwarfs: "Ducky" Medwick, Frankie "The Fordham Flash" Frisch, Leo "The Lip" Durocher, "Pepper" Martin, "Wild" Bill Hallahan, "Ripper" Collins, "Sunny" Jim Bottomley, and, of course, "Dizzy" and "Daffy" Dean. Together, they had captured the imagination of the American public.

First, however, they had trouble capturing the 1934 National League pennant. For, while the favorite of the fans might have been the Cards, the odds-on favorite of the experts was the New York Giants, the 1933 World Champions. Led by player-manager Bill Terry, outfielder Mel Ott and a pitch-ing staff that included Carl Hubbell, "Prince" Hal Schumacher and "Fat" Freddie Fitzsimmons, the Giants took off at the starting gate and by June 8 began to pull away from the field. By mid-August they had opened an eight-game lead over the floundering Cardinals, and the pennant race looked more like a cakewalk than a race.

The Cardinals, it seemed, were more intent on cutting up than catching up. They had a Dixieland band known as the "Mudcats," made up of washboards, kazoos and generally bad voices, played pranks (including dressing up in overalls and moving ladders and buckets into a posh hotel restaurant for so-called "repairs" and leaving the mess there during dinner hour), and even engaged in midget auto races. The heart of the team, as well as the biggest cutups, were Martin and Dean, who, when all was quiet, would grab the announcer's public-address microphone and entertain the spectactors with a wise-cracking account of the game, even calling on their teammates to take bows from the dugout. One time, during a crucial game in Cincinnati, Dean put a cake of ice on home plate to "cool off" his fastball. Another time, he built himself a bonfire in front of the dugout during a sweltering 100-degree day in St. Louis, and, covering himself with blankets, squatted down to "warm" his hands. It was enough to make a grown man laugh; or in the case of manager Frankie Frisch, cry.

The basic problem confronting Frisch was not just the unusually high spirits of the Cardinals (pronounced "spart" by Dean, as in "Spart of St. Louis"), but those of his star right-hander, Jay Hannah Dean. Dean was a man-boy who alternated between playing masterfully and playing mischievously. He would mimic his manager, both behind his back and in front of him. He would brag about his exploits and those of his brother ("Me and Paul will win 45 games this year"). And he would just be himself, not only slipping into his own idiomatic style of speech ("The way I see braggin' is when you do a lot of poppin' off and ain't got nothin' to back it up"), but also slipping away AWOL for days at a time.

Dean was an authentic American character. As a boy he had progressed to the second grade ("If I'd a went to the third grade, I'd a passed up my old man. And I didn't want to show Paw up"), spending the rest of his youth as a migratory cotton picker following the crops from one Southern state to another for 50¢ a day, all the while developing his back and his arm, but not his mind. (Something he acknowledged when he was inducted into baseball's Hall of Fame, thanking "the good Lord for giving me a good right arm, a strong back and a weak mind.")

However, his claims to a weak mind were suspect. He somehow always found the right rejoinder, providing the down-trodden with a chuckle at the expense of the mighty. (Once, when he had wandered into his hotel many hours after curfew and found the owner of the club waiting in the lobby for him, he assured him, "Well, I guess you and me will get the devil for this. But I won't say nothin' about it if you don't." Another time, he disputed a pitch with the plate umpire, but received no answer. "Why don't you answer my question?" he asked politely. "I did," the plate umpire replied, "I shook my head." "That's funny," said Dean, unable to resist the temptation, "I didn't hear nothin' rattle.") Ogden Nash, in his *ABC of Baseball Immortals*, best captured the quintessensial Dizzy:

> D is for Dean.
> The grammatical Diz,
> When they asked, Who's the tops?
> Said correctly, I is.

But Dean was known less for his delivery of a line than his delivery of a pitch. His fluid overhand motion had made him virtually unbeatable, as he mixed a blazing fastball with an excellent change of pace and a curve which, in Leo Durocher's words, "breaks like a ball falling off a pool table."

Together, they made Dean the attraction of the post-Ruthian era, a drawing card that Cardinal owner Sam Breadon capitalized on. According to sports writer Red Smith, Breadon would cancel a weekday game "if he so much as spat," rescheduling it as part of a Sunday doubleheader, and then "paper" the surrounding countryside throughout rural Missouri and southern Illinois with posters heralding the appearance of "DIZZY DEAN" who, it was announced in much smaller type, would "Pitch against _____ Sunday."

But if Dean was a show, he was also, more than once, a "no-show". Occasionally he would bridle at being shown off in exhibition games like a show dog, and go on strike. Once, after "Dizzy" and younger brother Paul (the sportswriter who named Paul "Daffy" did so more on balance than on facts, Paul being as quiet as "Dizzy" was gregarious) had lost a doubleheader to the Cubs on August 12, they both got lost. When Frisch counted heads that night, he saw nary a Dean head in sight. Hopping mad, he fined both brothers for their wildcat walkout, one of many. Hearing of the fines, the Deans refused to take the field when they rejoined the team two days later in Pittsburgh, and Frisch suspended them. "Dizzy" went on a rampage, tearing up two uniforms—one for benefit of insistent photographers—and stalked out of the clubhouse, determined to lay his case before Commissioner Landis.

Landis, however, was not impressed by the Deans' case, and admonished them as "willful little kids." Thoroughly chastened, they chased back home to pick up where they left off. And pick up they did. With one of the Deans pitching almost every day, the Cardinals were back into a pennant fight they had practically abandoned hopes of winning.

Still, despite winning seven of their next eight games, the week of Labor Day found them seven full games behind the front-running Giants. However, their pumpkin was about to turn into a carriage plus six, with the two trace horses the Deans. The day it turned was September 21, in a doubleheader against the same Brooklyn Dodgers that were now bedeviling Terry's Giants, getting even with Terry for his ill-fated off-season taunt, "Are the Dodgers still in the League?"

With the two brothers scheduled to pitch, Frisch was going over the Brooklyn batting order, player by player. Dizzy, however, was having none of the pregame strategy meeting, and after listening to every Frisch suggestion, finally said,

"This is silly, Frank. I've won 26 games already this season and it don't look exactly right for an infielder like you to be tellin' a star like me how I should pitch." Then, with Frisch fuming that he would "get his ears pinned back," he picked up his glove and shouted over his shoulder, "They ain't pinnin' Ol' Diz' ears back. I doubt if them Dodgers get a hit off either me or Paul today." (Earlier Dizzy had told a St. Louis writer, "Zachary and Benge will be pitching against one-hit and two-hit Dean today.")

And "danged" if Diz was just "braggin'." He had a no-hitter through 8⅔ innings and finished up with a tidy three-hit shutout. But in the nightcap, Paul went him three better, limiting the Dodgers to no hits to move the Cards to within three games of the top. In the clubhouse after the game, Dizzy came up to his younger brother and said, in a hurt tone, "Whyn't you tell Ol' Diz you were gonna pitch a no-hitter? If I'd a knowed that, I'd of pitched me one, too."

Still, they gave Frisch fits. When he ran into Boston Brave manager Casey Stengel during the last month of the season, he complained, "Case, I don't know what to do about them boys. They're driving me nuts." Casey asked how many games they had won. "Forty-two," Frisch replied. "Hell, you think you got trouble? I got two pitchers who lost 42 games between them."

The Deans were a brother act, to be sure. So much so that a third Dean brother, Elmer, served as a peanut vendor at Sportsman's Park in St. Louis, earning a reputation for his accurate and long throws.

It was that kind of a year, and with two games to go, the Giants stumbled—to the Dodgers, obviously—and the Cards clinched the pennant on Dean's thirtieth win, making him the last National Leaguer to reach that figure. His brother Paul won *only* 19, making good his spring training boast that "Me and Paul will win 45 games."

The Cardinals had won the pennant. Now it was on to the World Series and the Detroit Tigers, who, under their scrappy player-manager Mickey Cochrane, had won their first pennant in 25 years by a comfortable seven games over the Yankees.

The Tigers' pennant had been as much a surprise as St. Louis'. Mired in fifth place a year before—25 games behind the first-place Washington Senators—the Tigers had undergone some changes over the winter. Tiger owner Frank Navin had strengthened the team by sending outfielder Jonathon Stone to Washington for outfielder Leon "Goose" Goslin, and then gone into the market to get a manager. He had first offered the job to Babe Ruth, then being "retired" by the Yankees. But Ruth had told him he'd "see him" when he got back from a barnstorming trip to Japan. Feeling slighted, Navin didn't want to wait—especially for Ruth. And so, he approached Connie Mack. Mack, the "Mr. Chips of Baseball," was in the process, for the second time in his team's history, of breaking up the Philadelphia Athletics. The first time had been because of disappointment at their showing in the 1914 Series and his fear of a bidding war with the Federal League. This time, the reason was financial: he was $500,000 in debt. Mack passed the hat among his fellow owers, giving them players in return. The White Sox got Simmons, Haas and Dykes for $150,000. Grove, Walberg, Foxx and Bishop were gone—or going. All that reminded of one of baseball's greatest teams was catcher Mickey Cochrane. And Navin wanted him. He got him for $100,000 with one other player, catcher John

Pasek, and promptly named Cochrane manager of the Tigers.

Cochrane announced at the start of spring training that the Tigers would win the 1934 pennant. Navin scoffed at the comment, saying, "In no other sport does form run as true as it does in baseball. We finished fifth last year and the year before. With Cochrane catching and Goslin supplying added batting punch, we should be a bit stronger this year and, with luck, finish fourth. Forget this talk about winning a pennant. If the club lands in fourth place, I'll be perfectly satisfied."

Cochrane, of course, was correct. His astuteness in assessing his team's chances was matched only by his inspirational leadership on the field, where he instilled a contagious combativeness that made the Tigers what they hadn't been in years—a winner. So convincing was his performance that, while the Cardinals might have been first in the hearts of the fans, the Tigers were first in the hearts of the bookmakers, who installed them as favorites in the Series.

The Series was to be remembered as one of Dean, Dean and more Dean—with a little garbage thrown in. It started with Dizzy pitching an eight-hitter while his teammates gave him 13 and an 8–3 victory. The second game saw Detroit's ace, Lynwood "Schoolboy" Rowe—whom the Cardinals tried to bait by hollering "How'm I doing, Edna?" every chance they got, a reference to a remark Rowe had made on radio, meant for his girlfriend's ears alone—beat the Cardinals and Hallahan 3–2 in twelve innings. Game three was won by Paul Dean 4–1 over Tommy Bridges, to give the Cards a 2–1 lead in games. Game four was the Tigers' turn, as they got 13 hits off five St. Louis pitchers, none of whom was named Dean, to win 10–4.

However, Dizzy did make an appearance in the fourth inning of the fourth game, inserting himself as a pinch runner for the slow-footed catcher Virgil Davis, and promptly breaking up a double play by getting hit in the middle of the forehead by Billy Rogell's relay to first. Carried off the field semiconscious, Dean was rushed to the hospital for X-rays, but was released after, in his own words, "the doctors X-rayed my head and found nothing."

With the Series tied at two games apiece, Dizzy came back to pitch—headache and all—but gave up seven hits, three of them for extra bases, losing to the Tigers and Tommy Bridges, 3–1. The Tigers had the Series lead 3–2, with the last two games at home in the friendly confines of Briggs Stadium.

Game six saw Paul going for the Cards against the Tigers' 24-game winner, Schoolboy Rowe. Rowe had had four days' rest and, considering his effectiveness in game two, it was a foregone conclusion that the Series would be all over by the late afternoon of October 8. But when Cochrane walked into the clubhouse before the game, he found his star right-hander seated on a trunk, nursing his swollen right hand. Rowe told at least four different versions of what happened to his hand, none of which were verifiable. But whatever the reason, it affected his delivery, and even without the "How'm-I-doing, Ednas?" he was not the Rowe of four days earlier, losing 4–3 on Paul Dean's run-producing single in the seventh.

In the clubhouse afterwards, Dizzy was wrestling his younger brother to the ground, hollering for all to hear, "You're the greatest pitcher the Dean family ever had." Then he would pound everyone else on the back and begin all over. In the middle of this bedlam, a writer came up to interview Cardinals manager Frisch and asked who would start this seventh game: "Dean tomorrow—the other Dean?" Frisch,

head down between his legs, exhausted from the struggle, looked up and muttered, "If I last till tomorrow, maybe. It'll be Dean or 'Wild' Bill Hallahan."

Now the writer, John Carmichael of the Chicago *Daily News*, turned around to view a new source of excitement on the other side of the locker room, and espied Dizzy, wearing a pith helmet and swinging one of the inflatable rubber tigers, sold at Briggs Field, over his fellow teammates' heads. Carmichael said, "Wild horses couldn't keep Dean off that mound tomorrow, Frank."

It had been one of those disappointing, dreary, rainy afternoons for Tiger fans. One which prompted boxing manager Joe Jacobs—who had caught a cold and lost his bet on the Tigers as well—to comment "I shoulda stood in bed."

One Tiger, in fact, had—Mickey Cochrane. Cochrane had spent the night at the hospital for treatment of the spike wound he had suffered in the ninth inning of the previous day's game. Released on the morning of game seven, he named pitcher Eldon Auker, who had won the fourth game, as Detroit's starting pitcher. But it made "no never mind" to Dean who he was pitching against, or even that 40,902 fans were hooting at him as he warmed up. He just kept grinning and yelling to every Cardinal who passed by him during pregame practice, "I'll shut 'em out. Get me a couple of runs, that's all. I'll blank the blankety-blanks."

But for two innings nobody bothered to give Dizzy those runs. And so, in the top of the third, after "The All-American Out," Leo Durocher, had followed form and flied out, Dean took things into his own hands, hitting a clean single down the left-field line. When Goslin, figuring that most pitchers don't normally break their necks getting down to first, nonchalanted the ball, Dean took off for second, just beating Goslin's lobbed throw into the infield. That piece of base running might well have turned the Series around. The next man up, Pepper Martin, bounced a ball down the first-base line, exactly to the spot where, with Dean still on first, Tiger first baseman Hank Greenberg would have been standing, holding him on, and gotten at least a force out. But with Greenberg over at his normal position, the fleet Martin beat it out for an infield hit, putting men on first and third, with one out. Then Martin did what he had done many times previously to Cochrane, stole a base, and Auker had to walk the next man up, Jack Rothrock, to load the bases and set up a possible double play. The only trouble with that strategy was that the next man up, manager Frankie Frisch, hit a base-clearing double to right field, and Diz had his "couple of runs."

The Cardinals were to go on to score four more runs in the inning—Dizzy even chipping in a second hit, an infield single that drove in the last run of the inning—as Cochrane marched in his first corps of pitchers to turn off the Cardinal machine. But Auker, Rowe, Hogsett and Bridges were inadequate to the task and the Cardinals continued to score at will, adding two more in the sixth on a Pepper Martin single and a Joe Medwick triple.

Medwick's triple brought on the most uproarious moment —if not the most memorable one—in World Series history. For as he came sliding into third base, Tiger third baseman Marv Owen apparently spiked him, and Medwick lashed back with his foot, kicking at Owen. But as the smoke cleared, all that could be seen was Medwick, laying on his back atop the base, kicking at the hometown favorite. That did it. Tiger fans, who had sullenly sat through a long, frustrating afternoon, now had something to get worked up over. When Medrick went out to left field to take his place in the bottom of the sixth, he was greeted by the 18,000 fans in the wooden bleachers throwing cushions, bottles, lemons and even their shoes, with some trying to climb the 18-foot wire fence to get at him. (Medwick was to say later, "I knew why they threw it at me. What I can't figure out is why they brought it to the ballpark in the first place.")

Four times Medwick was called off the field, only to reassume his position and ignite an even higher crescendo of frustration and hate. Finally, after 20 minutes of this, Commissioner Landis called both managers and the two participants over to his box. He asked Medwick, "Did you kick him?" to which Medwick answered, "You're damned right, I did!" Then he turned to Owen and asked "Do you know any reason why Medwick should have made such an attack?" Owen said he did not. Landis then excused Medwick for the rest of the afternoon, silenced Frisch's protests and ordered the game to continue.

But the conclusion of the game was a foregone one. Dizzy Dean was to go on to win the most lopsided shutout in World Series history, 11–0, giving up only six hits, and finishing not only one of the greatest years any player has ever had—but also one of the greatest years any brothers have ever had.

It would only have been Deansian had Dizzy been able to carry through his original Series plan, one which he sought the help of Grantland Rice, the late dean of American sports writers, to carry out. Before the Series started, Diz had asked Granny if he could arrange to have Frisch let Dizzy pitch the entire series. "You can't possibly win four straight games," Rice had incredulously told the grinning pitcher standing before him. "I know I cain't," Diz had replied, "But I can win four out of five."

That was Dizzy Dean and that was 1934, a never-to-be-forgotten melding of a man and his times.

Official Souvenir Program

WORLD SERIES, 1934

●

Major League Advisory Council

HON. KENESAW M. LANDIS
Commissioner of Baseball

WM. HARRIDGE
President American League

JOHN A. HEYDLER
President National League

Detroit American Baseball Club Officials

FRANK J. NAVIN
President

WALTER O. BRIGGS
Vice-President

CHARLES F. NAVIN
Secretary

St. Louis National Baseball Club Officials

SAM BREADON
President

BRANCH RICKEY
Vice-President

CLARENCE F. LLOYD
Secretary

WM. O. DeWITT
Treasurer

LEADERSHIP

Mickey Cochrane's leadership has been an inspiring thing to watch throughout the season as the Tigers battled down the stretch to win the pennant. The men at White Star realized what that leadership would do for the Tigers 'way last spring when they backed their faith in Mickey and his men with cold cash to bring both the home and out of town games to you over the air.

It takes a leader to pick a leader that far ahead . . . and it always pays to follow a leader . . . and that's what you do when you make White Star headquarters for all your motoring needs. Mobilgas, Mobiloil, Mobilubrication, tires, batteries and accessories, and friendly White Star Service . . . at the Sign of the Flying Red Horse.

WHITE STAR REFINING COMPANY

A SOCONY-VACUUM COMPANY

Gordon Stanley Cochrane, known as Mickey to the public and Mike to ball players, is ranked by many as the greatest catcher of all times. He has never had a superior at working pitchers (as the records of the Detroit pitchers this year indicate), he is one of the best throwing catchers of all time, he has a life-time batting average of better than .320 and he is one of two catchers who were fast enough to be used as lead-off batters in the major leagues. Detroit bought him last winter, at the age of 31, for the sum of $100,000 cash and a player. The Detroit owners gambled "One hundred grand" that Cochrane would be a successful manager and this program is conclusive proof of his managerial success.

Cochrane took a squad of players whom few people believed could finish as high as fourth and developed them into the baseball sensations of the year. His team was chiefly composed of young men. Cochrane, Gehringer and Goslin are the only three who can be ranked as veterans. His success with the youngsters made the team champions of the league. Possessed of a magnetic personality, a rare and robust fighting spirit, a mad passion for victory, Cochrane's wild enthusiasm was infectious and he created a team that he always refers to as the "Battling Bengals." Several times it seemed that the "Battling Bengals" were on the verge of receding into the second division shell to which they had become accustomed these many years but each time Cochrane succeeded in leading them back to the high road.

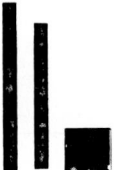

DETROIT TIGERS — American League Champions, 1934

TOP ROW—Carroll, Trainer; Willis, Bat Boy; Fischer, Pitcher; Crowder, Pitcher; Walker, Outfielder. THIRD ROW—Schuble, Infielder; Doljack, Outfielder; Gehringer, Second Base; Hamlin, Pitcher; Hogsett, Pitcher; Marberry, Pitcher; Goslin, Outfielder. SECOND ROW—York, Outfielder; Auker, Pitcher; Owen, Third Base; Hayworth, Catcher; Rogell, Shortstop; Sorrell, Pitcher; Bridges, Pitcher; Greenberg, First Base. BOTTOM ROW—Rowe, Pitcher; Clifton, Infielder; White, Outfielder; Cochrane, Catcher; Perkins, Coach; Baker, Coach; Fox, Outfielder.

ELDEN AUKER—There is generally an argument going on somewhere relative to Elden Auker's delivery. It is strictly underhand but is it as much underhand as Carl Mays' was? If Auker doesn't come as low to the ground as Carl Mays in his sweeping underhand delivery then he isn't more than an inch or so away. He is baseball's present submarine pitcher but he started his career as an overhand pitcher. That was in college. He also played football and was the best back in the Missouri Valley for two years. Bo McMillen, of Center College fame, was his coach. Auker broke his right shoulder in football and had to change himself over. He became an underhand pitcher. He was one of the Big Four of the Detroit pitching staff this year. His main accomplishment was holding Cleveland to one run in 27 innings, pitching 22 consecutive scoreless innings against them. This year was his first full one in the big leagues. He joined Detroit late in the 1933 season.

TOMMY BRIDGES' parents wanted him to be a doctor. His father is a doctor. His grandfather, great grandfather and great great grandfather were all doctors, known throughout the Tennessee countryside. Tommy did not want to be a doctor; he wanted to pitch baseball. That's what he has done extremely well for several years. A slender man, he pitches an astoundingly fast ball. He is said to have the best curve ball of any right-handed pitcher in the league. Like Grover Cleveland Alexander he depends upon the two deliveries. Wildness has been his lone handicap. On the days when he has control Bridges will win if his team gets him two or three runs. He has pitched three one-hit games in his career. In 1932 he lost his chance to pitch a perfect game against Washington when, after having retired the first 26 batters who faced him, a pinch hitter singled for the only hit. Bridges retired the next batter.

HERMAN CLIFTON—His Christian name is Herman Clifton and his home is in Cincinnati but they call him "Flea." It's his size, probably. He does not carry much poundage but there is great speed in his legs and he is a whirlwind on the bases. He won an important game for Detroit a few weeks ago by scoring the deciding run from second base on an infield out. He is an elegant fielder but has had only a few innings of play this year because the Detroit infielders insist upon playing every day. If given a chance Clifton would be a sensational fielder but his proper place is second base and a gent by the name of Gehringer looks after that position, so the Flea sits on the bench unless there is occasion to do a little streaking on the bases.

ALVIN CROWDER—Detroit got Crowder two months ago because nobody else wanted him. The other seven clubs thought that he was through as a big league pitcher. Washington twice asked waivers on him and the second time the Detroit players asked Mickey Cochrane to buy Crowder because they believed that he could come back. In response to the players' request Crowder was bought by Detroit and he was one of the team's great performers in the tightest spot of the pennant race. He started the last two Detroit-New York series, each time opposing Lefty Gomez. He won each game. In his last two games Crowder held opposing teams (one of them the Yankees) to one run. He never looked better in his life. He had as much stuff as ever. A smart pitcher, Crowder has everything in the way of stuff that a pitcher carries. He is one of the great "money" performers of baseball, always being at his best in the pinch.

CARL FISCHER—The blond left-hander Carl W. Fischer is extremely effective against at least two teams in the American League. Cleveland does not like to see him go to the box and neither does St. Louis. With any luck he would have been the first Detroit pitcher to beat Vernon Gomez. They had a great pitching duel in New York one Sunday in mid-summer and Gomez finally won out, 3 to 2. When Fischer has control he is a difficult pitcher to hit. He has a good fast ball and his curve is even better. At bat he is not much stronger than Johnny Broaca of the Yankees, who is reputed to be the weakest batter in the American League, but Mr. Fischer explains this by saying, "Pitchers aren't hired to hit." Mr. Fischer's specialty is pitching and he manages to do this very well on most of the occasions when he appears in the box.

FRANK DOLJACK is the only Slovak in the major leagues and, we are told, the only one in baseball. He is utility outfilder. One of the leading batters of minor league baseball Doljack has never been able to hit consistently in the American League and this is his one drawback. He is a very good outfielder and has the best throwing arm of any Detroit outfielder. He lacks the speed of White, Walker and Fox but he manages to get around very well and few balls ever get by him. He is a sure fielder on either grounders or flies. He is a good base-runner. His home is in Cleveland and he developed on the sandlots of that city. He was "prepped" for the major leagues in the American Association, where he was an outstanding star.

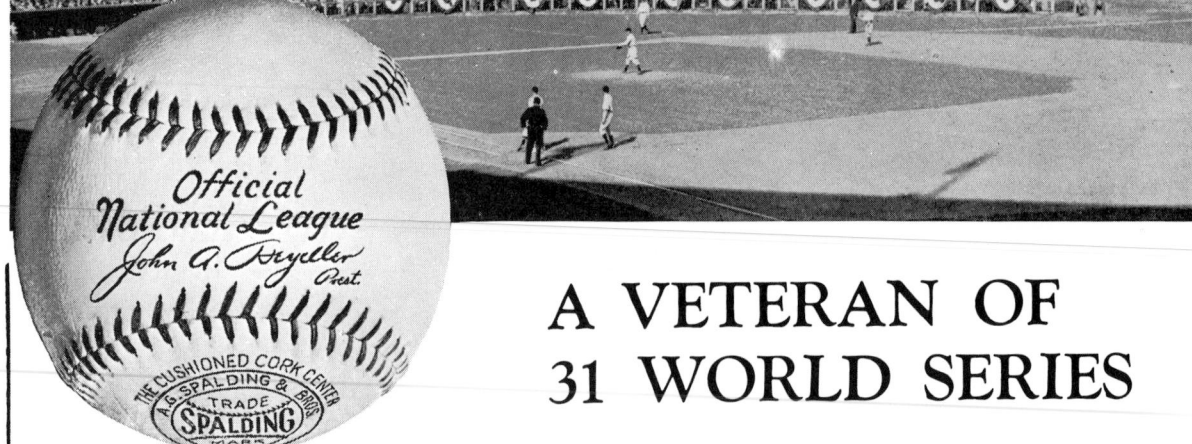

Leon Allen Goslin, who became "The Goose" as he grew older, is 34 and the oldest player on the Detroit team. He became a member last winter when Detroit secured him from Washington in exchange for Jonathan Stone. The owners wanted aggressiveness and Goslin is ultra-aggressive. Also, he carried a "first-division complex" and Detroit needed that. In the first two months of the season Goslin was one of two players who supplied the main driving force that established Detroit in the first division and elevated the team into a serious contender. The other player was Mickey Cochrane. Between them they managed to imbue others with their winning spirit.

Ervin Fox, first known as Peter the Fox and then as plain Pete, has played right field for Detroit nearly the entire season. He is very fast, a fine judge of fly balls and while his throwing arm is not as strong as it might be he still makes no mistakes in throwing. He covers plenty of ground. He rarely talks. He is either leading off the Detroit batting order or batting in eighth place, all depending upon whether Mickey Cochrane or Ray Hayworth is doing the catching. Pete is a little fellow but he manages to hit the ball a surprisingly long way. He is exceedingly fast on the bases and he runs with fine judgment. He is the least aggressive of the Detroit outfielders but he has a steadying influence and he never varies from a given pace. He is extremely dependable.

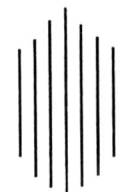

HENRY GREENBERG is playing his first full season in the major leagues but he has established himself as one of the great sluggers of baseball. He will come near averaging two bases per hit. His bat drove in the tieing or winning run in forty of Detroit's victories. An awkward fielder when he made his debut last season he has developed into one of the best fielding first basemen in the big leagues. He is a competitor of the finest type, adding a flaming spirit to his physical assets such as height, reach, wrist, forearm and shoulder power. He is still improving and will, within a few years, be rated as one of the best of all time.

CHARLES LEONARD GEHRINGER is the most graceful infielder since the days of Napoleon Lajoie. Like the great Frenchman he never wastes a motion. He is the perfect economist. Rated as the best second baseman of his time he is one of the game's leading batters as well as its best infielder. He executes every play with the "poetry of motion and perfection of form". His hands are among the surest that baseball has known and he has probably more range than any other second sacker. He is an almost perfect thrower. He has size, weight, strength, power, speed and agility. He is the ideal physical type for infield play. He ranks with the best of all time.

ROSTER OF THE TIGERS, 1934

Player's Name	Date of Birth and Place	Height	Weight	Bats	Throws	Home Address
PITCHERS						
AUKER, ELDEN	Sept. 21, 1910, Norcatur, Kan.	6'2"	194	R	R	Norcatur, Kansas
BRIDGES, THOS.	Dec. 28, 1906, Gordonsville, Tenn.	5'10¾"	155	R	R	Gordonsville, Tenn.
CROWDER, ALVIN	Jan. 11, 1901, Winston-Salem, N.C.	5'10"	170	L	R	Winston-Salem, N. C.
FISCHER, CHAS. W.	Nov. 5, 1905, Medina, N. Y.	6'	180	R	L	Medina, N. Y.
HAMLIN, LUKE D.	July 3, 1906, Terris Center, Mich.	6'	168	L	R	Lansing, Mich.
HOGSETT, ELON C.	Nov. 2, 1903, Brownell, Kan.	6'	195	L	L	Daytona Beach, Fla.
MARBERRY, FRED	Nov. 30, 1899, Streetman, Texas	6'2"	210	R	R	Corsicana, Tex.
ROWE, LYNWOOD T.	Jan. 11, 1912, Waco, Texas	6'4"	205	R	R	El Dorado, Ark.
SORRELL, VICTOR	April 9, 1902, Morrisville, N. C.	5'10"	170	R	R	Raleigh, N. C.
CATCHERS						
COCHRANE, GORDON S., Mgr.	April 6, 1903, Bridgewater, Mass.	5'10½"	180	L	R	Cynwyd, Pa.
HAYWORTH, RAY H.	Jan. 29, 1905, High Point, N. C.	6'	180	R	R	High Point, N. C.
YORK, RUDOLPH P.	Aug. 17, 1913, Ragland, Ala.	6'1"	209	R	R	Atco, Ga.
INFIELDERS						
CLIFTON, HERMAN E.	Dec. 12, 1911, Cincinnati, Ohio	5'10"	160	R	R	Cincinnati, O.
GEHRINGER, CHAS. L.	May 11, 1903, Fowlerville, Mich.	5'11"	180	L	R	Detroit, Mich.
GREENBERG, HENRY	Jan. 1, 1911, New York, N. Y.	6'3½"	210	R	R	New York, N. Y.
OWEN, MARVIN J.	Mar. 22, 1908, San Jose, Calif.	6'1"	175	R	R	San Jose, Calif.
ROGELL, WM. G.	Nov. 24, 1904, Springfield, Ill.	5'10½"	163	R&L	R	Detroit, Mich.
SCHUBLE, HENRY G.	Nov. 1, 1906, Houston, Texas	5'8"	160	R	R	Houston, Tex.
OUTFIELDERS						
DOLJACK, FRANK	Oct. 5, 1910, Cleveland, Ohio	5'11"	175	R	R	Cleveland, Ohio
FOX, ERVIN	Mar. 8, 1909, Evansville, Ind.	5'11"	165	R	R	Evansville, Ind.
GOSLIN, LEON	Oct. 16, 1901, Salem, N. J.	5'11½"	185	L	R	Salem, N. J.
WALKER, GERALD H.	Mar. 19, 1909, Gulfport, Miss.	5'11"	185	R	R	Hattiesburg, Miss.
WHITE, JOYNER	June 1, 1909, Red Oak, Ga.	5'10½"	160	L	R	College Park, Ga.

ROSTER OF THE CARDINALS, 1934

Player's Name	Date of Birth and Place	Height	Weight	Bats	Throws	Home Address
PITCHERS						
CARLETON, JAMES O.	Aug. 19, 1906, Comachine, Texas	6'1½"	176	R	R	Fort Worth, Tex.
DEAN, JEROME H.	Jan. 16, 1911, Holdenville, Okla.	6'3¾"	189	R	R	Bradenton, Fla.
DEAN, PAUL	Aug. 14, 1913, Holdenville, Okla.	6'3"	192	R	R	Bradenton, Fla.
HAINES, JESSE JOSEPH	July 22, 1893, Clayton, O.	6'	180	R	R	Phillipsburg, O.
HALLAHAN, WILLIAM	Aug. 4, 1904, Binghamton, N. Y.	5'10½"	170	R	L	Binghamton, N. Y.
MOONEY, JAMES I.	Sept. 4, 1906, Mooresburg, Tenn.	5'10"	168	R	L	Mooresburg, Tenn.
WALKER, WILLIAM H.	Oct. 7, 1903, E. St. Louis, Ill.	6'1"	190	R	L	E. St. Louis, Ill.
VANCE, ARTHUR C. "DAZZY"	March 4, 1893, Des Moines, Iowa.	6'1"	205	R	R	Homasassa, Fla.
CATCHERS						
DAVIS, VIRGIL L.	Dec. 20, 1904, Birmingham, Ala.	6'1"	197	R	R	Birmingham, Ala.
DeLANCEY, WILLIAM P., Jr.	Nov. 28, 1911, Greensboro, N. C.	5'11½"	185	L	R	Greensboro, N. C.
HEALEY, FRANCIS	Sept. 9, 1911, Holyoke, Mass.	5'9½"	175	R	R	Holyoke, Mass.
INFIELDERS						
COLLINS, JAMES A.	March 30, 1905, Altoona, Pa.	5'9½"	165	R&L	L	Rochester, N. Y.
CRAWFORD, CLIFFORD R.	Jan. 28, 1902, Society Hill, S. C.	5'11"	178	L	R	Columbus, O.
DUROCHER, LEO E.	July 27, 1906, W. Springfield, Mass.	5'6"	165	R	R	Cincinnati, O.
FRISCH, FRANK F., Mgr.	Sept. 9, 1898, New York, N. Y.	5'11"	165	R&L	R	New Rochelle, N. Y.
MARTIN, JOHN LEONARD	Feb. 29, 1904, Temple, Okla.	5'8"	170	R	R	Oklahoma City, Okla.
WHITEHEAD, BURGESS	June 29, 1910, Tarboro, N. C.	5'10½"	170	R	R	Lewiston, N. C.
OUTFIELDERS						
FULLIS, CHARLES PHILIP	Feb. 27, 1904, Girardville, Pa.	5'9½"	170	R	R	Girardville, Pa.
MEDWICK, JOSEPH M.	Nov. 24, 1911, Carteret, N. J.	5'9"	180	R	R	Carteret, N. J.
ORSATTI, ERNEST RALPH	Sept. 8, 1904, Los Angeles, Cal.	5'7¾"	154	L	L	Los Angeles, Cal.
ROTHROCK, JOHN H., Jr.	March 14, 1906, Long Beach, Cal.	6'	180	R&L	R	Columbus, O.

LUKE HAMLIN—His family name is Hamlin but his first name is not Luke. He has no first name. They named him L. D. when he was born but he never found out what the "L" or the "D" stood for. He was told they did not stand for anything—just L. D. When he entered the Texas League they said he would have to have a name, the L. D. would not do. They told him he ought to be called Luke and he said he thought Luke as good as anything if they paid him on time. They paid him on time and he has been Luke ever since. He is a slender right-hander with a very deceptive fast ball. They call that sort of fast ball delivery a "sneaker" in baseball because the ball is on top of the batter before he realizes it. Hamlin has a fair curve ball and his control is generally good.

RAY HAYWORTH—With Mickey Cochrane catching nearly every game, Ray Hayworth has had little chance this year. He was, for seasons, Detroit's first-string catcher. He is an excellent backstop. He has a very strong throwing arm and he is accurate. There was never any wild base-running in games that Hayworth caught. And he is an accomplished batter. He is the ideal type of hitter since he puts a lot of power behind his swing and drives the ball through. He is calm and very steady. No catcher in the game today has better form than Hayworth. Pitchers like to work with him. He comes from North Carolina, a state that has given several players to the Detroit roster. As proof of his mechanical skill it need only be said that he holds the big league record for consecutive innings by a catcher without a fielding error.

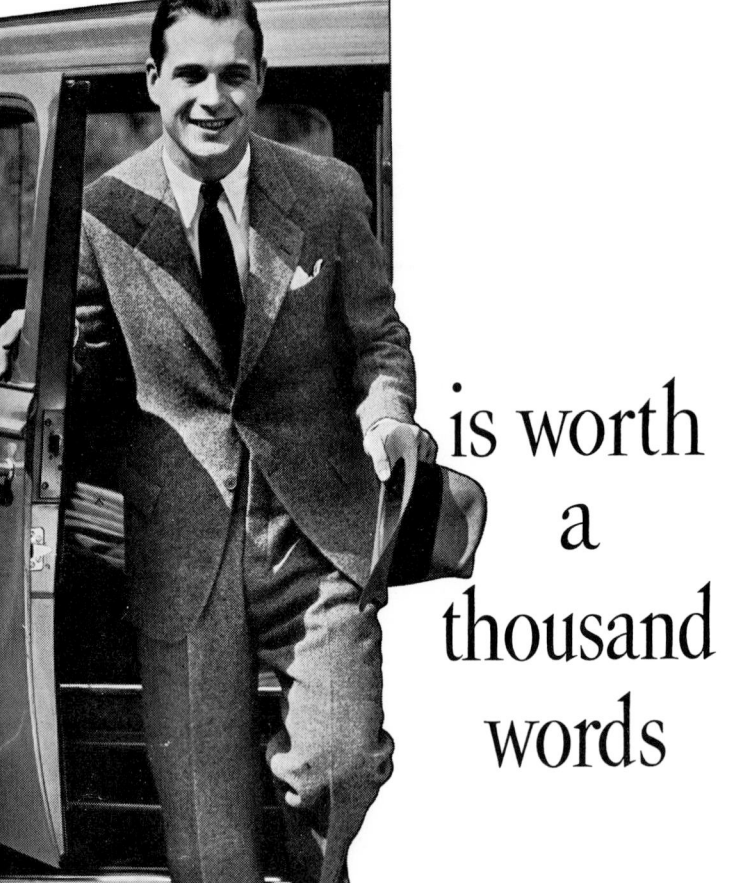

*O*ne ride

is worth
a
thousand
words

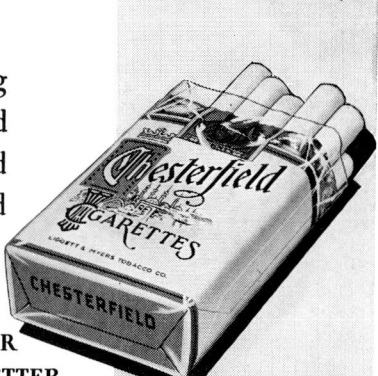
DETROIT AMERICANS

DETROIT		1	2	3	4	5	6	7	8	9	10	AB	R	BH	PO	A	E
Scr. Bd. No.	Uniform No.																
1 White, cf	(25)																
8 Cochrane, c	(3)																
9 Hayworth, c	(23)																
2 Gehringer, 2b	(2)																
3 Greenberg, 1b	(5)																
4 Goslin, lf	(4)																
5 Rogell, ss	(7)																
6 Owen, 3b	(8)																
7 Fox, rf	(12)																
	, p																

11 Rowe (14)	16 Marberry (11)	23 Hamlin (20)	112 Clifton (24)
12 Bridges (10)	17 Fisher (15)	49 York (19)	122 Walker (6)
14 Auker (13)	18 Hogsett (17)	61 DolJack (26)	Baker (32)
15 Crowder (16)	22 Sorrell (18)	71 Schuble (22)	Perkins (31)

Copyright 1934 by Detroit Baseball Co.

ST. LOUIS NATIONALS

ST. LOUIS Scr. Bd. No. Uniform No.	1	2	3	4	5	6	7	8	9	10	AB	R	BH	PO	A	E
1 Martin, 3b (1)																
2 Rothrock, rf (6)																
3 Frisch, 2b (3)																
4 Medwick, lf (7)																
5 Collins, 1b (12)																
8 Davis, c (8) 9 DeLancey, c (9)																
6 Orsatti, cf (5)																
7 Durocher, ss (2)																
p																

11 J. Dean	(17)	16 Walker	(18)	49 Healey	(27)
12 Carleton	(15)	17 Mooney	(28)	61 Fullis,	(4)
14 Hallahan	(22)	18 Vance	(19)	71 Whitehead	(14)
15 Haines	(16)	22 P. Dean	(21)	112 Crawford	(11)

Gonzales (25)
Wares (26)

1907 Tiger
Pennant
Winners

1908 Tiger
Pennant
Winners

1909 Tiger
Pennant
Winners

FRED MARBERRY—This is Fred Marberry's second season with Detroit. Before that he was with Washington. He has appeared in two world series. They call him Firpo and he acquired the nickname at Washington, where they nicknamed him after Luis Angel Firpo, the Argentinian giant who failed to take the heavyweight championship from Jack Dempsey by a fluke in refereeing. Marberry was noted as baseball's greatest relief pitcher while he was with Washington. He has been both starting and relief pitcher for Detroit. He has a peculiar delivery, throwing the lead foot high into the air when he winds up. He still has plenty of speed on his fast one. He is very aggressive and a great competitor. He loves to win and he bears down with everything at his command when he pitches. He is a Texan of heroic proportions, as his nickname indicates.

ELON C. HOGSETT has been called "Chief" ever since he entered organized ball, and whenever the gods of the bleachers catch sight of him warming up they cut loose with what is intended to be a series of Indian war whoops. This is Hogsett's reception in all cities of the American League circuit but privately he insists that he is not an Indian while a native philosophy prompts him to view with calm the public insistence that he is one of the original Americans. He pitches with his left arm, delivers a fine change of pace and a good curve ball, and is noted chiefly for his poise and the ease and grace of his delivery. A sidearm pitcher, he is baseball "poison" for several teams but illness has handicapped him in the last two years. However, at present, Hogsett is back in form.

Marvin Owen—They call him Merv but his name is Marvin and he belongs to the California Owen family. There is no "s" attached to the family name but he never frets when reporters insist upon adding the "s." He won a pennant and "little world series" for Newark in 1932 but he showed little with Detroit last year because he was ill. They wanted to get another third baseman this spring but failed and so they had to use Owen. That was lucky for Detroit. He is probably the best third baseman in the league this year. A great fielder, he has the most powerful hands found on any American League infield, and the largest. He can hold seven baseballs in either hand. He is one of the team's best hitters and a very dangerous gent when there are men on bases. Hitting safely with the bases jammed is his specialty. He has a magnificent throwing arm and plays short hops better than any other third baseman.

Bill Rogell (his baptismal name is Wilhelm and not William) traveled the baseball highways and byways for several years before he became a big league regular. The Boston Red Sox had him and shipped him back to the minors. Detroit bought him, tried him, and also sent him back. A few years later Detroit was in need of a shortstop and the best man in all the minor leagues was Rogell, the same lad whom they had discarded. So they bought him back and he has been a regular since. He has batted better than .300 during most of the current season and several astute gentlemen have picked him as the best shortstop in the American League this year. No shortstop equals him playing a bad hop and he has an excellent throwing arm. He is a good base-runner and a very capable lead-off man although he has not been used in the No. 1 batting position this year.

HENRY GEORGE SCHUBLE, and this is probably the first time that his full Christian name was ever published because he has been known all through life as plain Heinie, has been with the Detroit team for several years as utility infielder. He came from Texas and he goes back there each winter. He likes the state. Schuble is an awkward fielder and an awkward base-runner but he is surprisingly fast both in fielding and running bases. He lacks weight but he has good timing and drives a ball a long way. Since only one Detroit infielder has missed a single game this year (and that one being Henry Greenberg) Heinie has had no chance to play. He appeared a few times as pinch hitter and acted as substitute runner a few times but he has made himself useful in coaching and working pitchers.

LYNWOOD ROWE—Four years ago he was pitching for a Sunday School nine in the then unrecognized El Dorado, Ark., and today, at the age of 22 and in his third year in organized baseball and his second year in the major leagues, Lynwood Rowe has made his name a household word. Known also as "Schoolhouse" and "Schoolyard" he is best known as "Schoolboy". Six feet four inches tall and perfectly proportioned this young giant out of Arkansas appeals to the imagination as few pitchers ever have. He won 16 games in a row this summer and tied the American League record held jointly until this year by Walter Johnson, Joe Wood and Bob Grove. He has an explosive curve ball, dazzling speed and probably the best change of pace in baseball. He won four of his games by his hitting as well as his pitching. He should become one of the immortals of the game. But, comparatively limited as his experience is, Rowe this summer drew more people to games in which he appeared than any other pitcher before his time.

VICTOR SORRELL, the little right hander, for some dim and vague reason, carries the nickname of Baby. He is one of the few pitchers in the game who wears spectacles while pitching. (A number of the boys wear them in the evening while reading the box scores, pitching and batting averages). Sorrell, a North Carolinian, is probably the unluckiest pitcher who ever worked for Detroit. He is a player of great courage and considerable stuff but his team rarely gets any runs for him and the opposing team is generally lucky at bat when Sorrell is pitching. His sliding fast ball is a very hard delivery to hit. He has a good curve ball and, as a rule, his control is excellent. He is one of the veterans of the Detroit staff.

GERALD (GEE) WALKER is one of the few players baseball had ever known who is too aggressive. His mad desire to win has caused him to make mistakes and these mistakes have kept him from playing regularly. He is one of the fastest men in the game and he is a splendid batter but he has never succeeded in harnessing his speed. He is a great competitor and his high spirit and dashing style make him one of the main favorites of Navin Field. He has lost a few games for Detroit but he has also won a considerable number. He has everything except control over his aggressive impulses and as soon as he becomes settled to a point where he curbs his base-running he will be one of the game's great stars. He has all the mechanical skill that is demanded in the top ranking player.

Rudy York joined the Detroit team late this season. He came from Fort Worth, in the Texas League. He is part Cherokee Indian and his home is in Atco, **Ga.** **He was a** sensation in the Texas League, especially when he played in Tulsa, Oklahoma. The Indians would leave the reservations and come to the ball park to see Rudy play. They brought him gifts and hailed him as a great chief. He is a big man and powerful. He is not fast enough for the big league outfields but York is a versatile player. **He** held down third base in the minors and he also did considerable catching. **He can play** anywhere. He was noted for his slugging ability and his long hits made him a star attraction in the Texas belt. He will probably be developed into a catcher by Detroit and his reputation should rival that of Chief Myers, the Indian who caught for the New York Giants for several years.

Joyner White—One of the highlights of the season was the over-night development of Joyner White, better known as Jo-Jo, the Tigah Man, or plain Jo-Jo. A frail outfielder who lacked stamina last year and could not play for stretches longer than four or five days, White suddenly became one of the best outfielders in the league. A very fine fielder, with a strong and accurate throwing arm, he made himself into one of the most important cogs of the Detroit attack. In the last half of the season he established himself as the best base-runner in the league and while not a strong hitter he was still an invaluable batter because he managed to get on the bases frequently. He is a hard man to pitch to and, because of his speed, he succeeds in beating out many bunts and reaches first on infield bobbles.

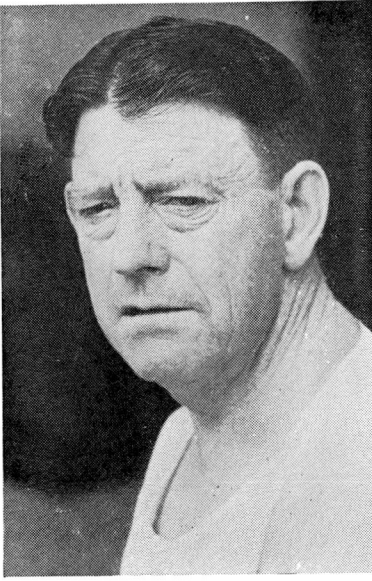

DELMAR BAKER came to Detroit a year ago last spring to become assistant to Stanley R. Harris, then manager of the Detroit team. When Harris resigned and Gordon Stanley Cochrane succeeded him he appointed Baker as one of his two assistants. Del Baker caught ball for Detroit in the days of Hugh Ambrose Jennings and he has been with the Detroit club in the capacity of scout, minor league manager, and more recently coach, almost ever since he quit being a catcher here. He handled several of the present Detroit stars in their minor league days. He is generally rated as the No. 1 coach of the major leagues, a fine developer of players and a tutor to the younger members of the Detroit team.

DENNIS CARROLL has been trainer of the Detroit team for the last few years but he was known to the major leagues for more than 20 years before he joined Detroit. Carroll, as trainer of the San Francisco baseball team, became recognized as the best man at his position in baseball, minor or major. Big leaguers used to travel to San Francisco to have Carroll restore their arms or legs and before he ever saw a major league park he had treated most of the stars of baseball. The depression made a trainer a luxury in the minors and Carroll came to Detroit. He was, in his youth, one of the best amateur boxers in the country. Later he became a swimmer and swam anchor on the team that set the world relay mark. He coached swimmers and boxers before he turned his attention to baseball.

RALPH (CY) PERKINS—When Mickey Cochrane joined the Philadelphia Athletics as a recruit he found Ralph (Cy) Perkins installed as a regular catcher. Cochrane succeeded Perkins mainly because of the coaching Perkins gave him. They have been inseparable friends ever since except during the period when Perkins was an assistant of Joe McCarthy in New York. When Cochrane signed to manage Detroit Perkins resigned as McCarthy's assistant at New York and joined Cochrane again. He and Del Baker have helped Cochrane develop Detroit into a pennant winner. Perkins was one of the leading catchers of his day. He has worked with some of the best pitchers in baseball. Gifted with a ready wit Perkins always helped break the tension during the thick of Detroit's pennant fight.

Detroit's Baseball History

Detroit's professional base ball history goes back to 1881. That was the year the city entered the old National League with a team that finished fourth.

For eight seasons Detroit remained in the National League, winning the pennant in 1887 under the management of William H. Watkins and topping off the achievement with a victory over the St. Louis Browns in the World Series.

The championship club that Watkins led is best remembered for the batting feats of the Big Four—Rowe, Richardson, White and Brouthers, all of whom were purchased from Buffalo the previous winter.

Strangely enough, Detroit dropped out of the National League immediately after its most spectacular success. The club owners decided that the city did not have the population to support a big league club and the franchise was transferred.

Until 1894 Detroit was not represented in organized Base Ball. When the old Western League was formed that year, Detroit became a member and kept its franchise until the American League was launched by the late Ban Johnson in 1900.

This city has been continuously a part of the American League since its inception. It has had nine managers, four pennants and hundreds of ball players, including Tyrus Raymond Cobb, the greatest of them all.

George Tweedy Stallings, one of the glamorous figures of the game, was Detroit's first manager in the American League. He had charge in 1900 and in 1901.

When Stallings resigned in the middle of the 1902 campaign, he was succeeded by the man who had been assistant, Frank Dwyer. Dwyer handled the club only part of one season and it finished seventh. A change was demanded and in 1903 Detroit started under Edward G. Barrow, afterward manager of the Boston Red Sox, president of the International League and now general manager of the New York Yankees.

Barrow directed the Tigers in 1903 and 1904. He was replaced in 1905 by Bill Armour, who held the position for two years and to some extent laid the foundation of the flag-winning combination that flowered under Hughie Jennings.

Jennings followed Armour in 1907 and his success was immediate. He produced pennant winners in the first three years of his reign and in each of the following years his club was in the fight, as it usually was during his long tenure as boss of the Bengals.

The Tigers under Jennings were beaten in the World Series of 1907 and 1908 by the Chicago Cubs. In 1909 they lost to Pittsburgh in a series that presented the greatest players of each league—Cobb and Hans Wagner, the celebrated shortstop of the Pirates.

Besides Cobb, Jennings had some players whose names are illustrious in base ball history. Wild Bill Donovan is generally regarded as the greatest pitcher Detroit ever had. George Mullin, Ed. Killian, Edgar Willett, and Eddie Summers were other members of the staff. Claude Rossman, Germany Schaefer, Charlie O'Leary, George Moriarty, Bill Couglin, Jim Delahanty, Tom Jones and Donie Bush were at one time or another his infielders. Sam Crawford, a natural slugger, Davey Jones, Matty McIntyre and others patrolled the outfield. The colorful Charlie Schmidt and Oscar Stanage were his catchers.

When Jennings at last laid aside the reins after the disastrous season of 1920, Cobb was promoted from the position of journeyman outfielder to one that required him both to play and to manage. He filled the dual role until the end of the 1926 season. He never had a championship team but in the six years of his leadership, Detroit finished four times in the first division and once landed in second place.

When Cobb stepped aside, George Moriarty removed his umpire's mask and chest protector and took his place. He piloted the Tigers for two years after which he was replaced by Stanley Raymond Harris, whose conspicuous success at Washington recommended him for the berth. Harris remained as Top Tiger through five years and developed some of the young players that grace the present championship roster. He resigned last fall and Mickey Cochrane was purchased from the Philadelphia Athletics for $100,000 to succeed him. Cochrane's triumph is so fresh in memory that it hardly needs to be reviewed in detail. Suffice it to say, that through his magnetic leadership and high grade mechanical skill, he brought the Tigers back on the top after 25 years of wandering in the wastelands.

Associated Press Photo

FRANK FRANCIS FRISCH (plain Frankie Frisch to a few million baseball followers) was a manager two months before Mickey Cochrane was appointed head of the Detroit team. Frisch succeeded Charles (Gabby) Street as boss of the Cardinals late last season.

Frisch has sixteen seasons of major league competition behind him and he is now engaged in his seventh world series. He is one of the few players born in New York City and the Giants were the club that Frisch joined originally. John J. McGraw signed him and he spent eight years on the Giants' infield, playing second base, shortstop and third base. McGraw traded him to St. Louis after the 1926 season and he has been with the Cardinals ever since.

He is regarded as the best second baseman in the National League. A great fielder, he is also a very dependable hitter. He has thirteen seasons of .300 batting behind him and a lifetime average that is well over .300.

What attracted McGraw to Frisch was the player's aggressiveness. He belongs to the fighting type. A great competitor, Frisch became invaluable because of his speed and quickness. He covers much territory around second, is equally good going to his left or right, a great one to come in on slow-hit balls and throw while off balance, and he can go deep into the rightfield fair or foul territory. Added to his mechanical ability is a rare intelligence.

Frisch, like Cochrane, pulled a pennant out of his bag in his first full managerial season, where Cochrane had his team on top nearly all season long, Frisch had to come from behind in a nerve-racking finish. One week before the season closed few people in St. Louis believed that the Cardinals had a chance to win, but Frisch managed miraculously to pull them through, making up more ground in one week than he had been able to make up in five months previously.

This stretch drive of the Cardinals, "ridden" by Frisch, must be accepted as one of the noteworthy performances of modern baseball.

JEROME (DIZZY) DEAN—Few people know him as Jerome Dean. Far and wide he is known as "Dizzy" and he is the best pitcher in the National League. He has a fast ball, a curve and a change of pace. He knows how to pitch. He is a "natural," pitching by instinct and not by design. He automatically does the right thing. He is one of the outstanding characters of sport, a pitcher who tells you that he is the best in the game and that only one other is near his class. The other one is Paul Dean, the young brother of "Dizzy." A very smart performer when he is on the rubber, "Dizzy" is one of the most eccentric of men when off the infield. On blistering hot days (and days get hot in St. Louis) he builds bonfires in front of the dugout, wraps himself in blankets and sits before the fire, warming his hands. That is one of his stunts. He has many more. But the guy can pitch.

PAUL DEAN—Known chiefly as "Dizzy's younger brother," Paul Dean may become so good that in years to come "Dizzy" Dean will be known as Paul Dean's "older brother." The younger Dean was ballyhooed in the major leagues by brother "Dizzy," who kept telling people that Paul was a much better pitcher than "Dizzy." It is true that Paul has a "swifter" fast ball than "Dizzy," but his curve and change of pace are not so good. Still, he is young and is constantly improving and no one can guess how far he will go. He pulled one for the book recently when he pitched a no-hit game against Brooklyn. On the same afternoon "Dizzy" pitched a three-hit shutout. The Deans have pitched five double-headers this year and three times they won both games. Their double shutout against Brooklyn is their most noteworthy performance. They are the first two brothers appearing on the same big league staff.

JOHN LEONARD MARTIN — In 1931 John Leonard Martin was so obscure that the Philadelphia Athletics did not even notice him when they were scouting the St. Louis Cardinals preparatory to the world series. But when the seventh game had been completed Martin, nicknamed "Pepper," stood out as the man who won the world championship for the Cardinals. He made twelve hits in twenty-four times at bat for the astounding world series average of .500, and he stole five bases. His hitting and base-running represented the hub of the Cardinals' attack. Few players have ever flashed into prominence with either the speed or the brilliance of Martin. Since nothing was expected of him he was not under the same pressure as his mates and he arose to the opportunities as few men ever have. He gave one of the greatest exhibitions in world series history.

JOE MEDWICK—In 1932 Joe Medwick was the best outfielder in the Texas League and Ervin Fox was rated the second best. In the spring of 1933 each came to the Big Tent, Medwick as a member of the St. Louis Cardinals outfield and Fox as a Detroit outfielder. Each jumped into the regular lineup on his arrival in the major leagues. Medwick continues to hold an edge over Fox. He is one of the best hitters in the National League and he gets a lot of power behind his swings. He is a better hitter than Fox but Fox is a better fielder than Medwick. Joe came to the big leagues with the nickname of "Ducky". The boys have elaborated upon this and call him "Ducky Wucky". But the nickname is a poor description of Medwick, who is a hard-going gent at bat and on the bases. His fielding, while not as good as it might be, is still not bad.

We were with the Tigers all season as

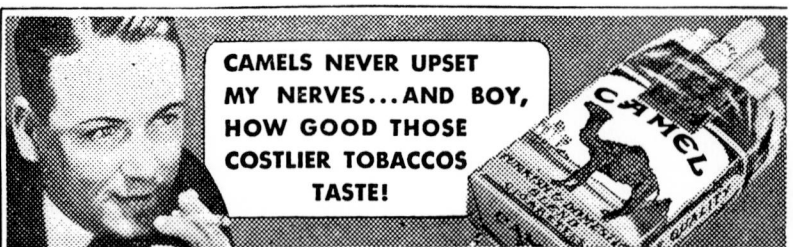

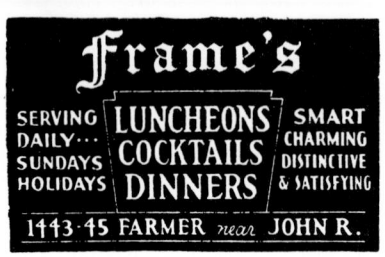

Official American League Schedule, 1934

Follow	AT CHICAGO	AT ST. LOUIS	AT DETROIT	AT CLEVELAND	AT WASHINGTON	AT PHILADELPHIA	AT NEW YORK	AT BOSTON
CHICAGO	*the*	April 27, 28, 29 July 30, 31, Aug. 1, 2 Aug. 31, 31, Sept. 1, 2	April 24, 25, 26 June 8, 9, 10 June 28 Aug. 3, 4, 5 Sept. 26	May 29, 30, 30, 31 July 5, 6, 7, 8 Sept. 28, 29, 30	May 6, 7, 8, 9 June 12, 13, 14, 15 Aug. 18, 19, 21	May 3, 4, 5 June 16, 17, 18, 19 Aug. 14, 15, 16, 17	May 10, 11, 12 June 24, 25, 26, 27 Aug. 26, 27, 28, 29	May 13, 14, 15 June 20, 21, 22, 23 Aug. 22, 23, 24, 25
ST LOUIS	April 20, 21, 22 June 5, 6, 7 July 4, 4 Aug. 10, 11, 12	*Tigers*	April 30, May 1, 2 July 6, 7, 8 Aug. 7, 8, 9 Sept. 29, 30	April 17, 18, 19 June 8, 9, 10 Aug. 3, 4, 5 Sept. 25, 26	May 10, 11, 12 June 24, 25, 26, 27 Aug. 26, 27, 28, 29	May 13, 14, 15 June 20, 21, 22, 23 Aug. 22, 23, 24, 25	May 6, 7, 8, 9 June 12, 13, 14, 15 Aug. 18, 19, 21	May 3, 4, 5 June 16, 17, 18, 19 Aug. 14, 15, 16, 17
DETROIT	April 17, 18, 19 June 1, 2, 3 July 27, 28, 29 Sept. 3, 3	May 29, 30, 30, 31 June 29, 30, July 1 Sept. 21, 22, 23, 24	*with*	April 20, 21, 22 July 2, 3 July 31, Aug. 1, 2 Aug. 30, Sept. 1, 2	May 13, 14, 15 June 20, 21, 22, 23 Aug. 22, 23, 24, 25	May 10, 11, 12 June 24, 25, 26, 27 Aug. 26, 27, 28, 29	May 3, 4, 5 June 16, 17, 18, 19 Aug. 14, 15, 16, 17	May 6, 7, 8, 9 June 12, 13, 14, 15 Aug. 18, 19, 21
CLEVELAND	April 30, May 1 June 29, 30, July 1 Aug. 7, 8, 9 Sept. 21, 22, 23	April 24, 25, 26 June 1, 2, 3 July 27, 28, 29 Sept. 3, 3	April 27, 28, 29 June 5, 6, 7 July 4, 4 Aug. 10, 11, 12	*Salsinger*	May 3, 4, 5 June 16, 17, 18, 19 Aug. 14, 15, 16, 17	May 6, 7, 8, 9 June 12, 13, 14, 15 Aug. 18, 19, 21	May 13, 14, 15 June 20, 21, 22, 23 Aug. 22, 23, 24, 25	May 10, 11, 12 June 24, 25, 26, 27 Aug. 26, 27, 28, 29
WASHINGTON	May 26, 27, 28 July 23, 24, 25, 26 Sept. 9, 10, 11, 12	May 23, 24, 25 July 19, 20, 21, 22 Sept. 5, 6, 7, 8	May 20, 21, 22 July 11 July 16, 17, 18 Sept. 17, 18, 19, 20	May 17, 18, 19 July 12, 13, 14, 15 Sept. 17, 18, 19, 20	*Daily*	April 20, 21, 22 July 2, 3 July 31, Aug. 1, 2 Sept. 22, 23, 24	May (30), (50), 31 July 5, 6, 7, 8 Aug. 30, 31 Sept. 7, 2	April 17, 18, 19, 19 June 8, 9, 10 Aug. 4, 5 Sept. 25, 26
PHILADELPHIA	May 17, 18, 19 July 12, 13, 14, 15 Sept. 17, 18, 19, 20	May 20, 21, 22 July 16, 17, 18 Sept. 13, 14, 15, 16	May 23, 24, 25 July 19, 20, 21, 22 Sept. 5, 6, 7, 8	May 26, 27, 28 July 23, 24, 25, 26 Sept. 9, 10, 11, 12	April 27, 28, 29 June 5, 6, 7 July (4), (4) Aug. 10, 11, 12	*in The*	April 24, 25, 26 June 8, 9, 10 Aug. 3, 4, 5 Sept. (3), (3)	April 30, May 1, 2 July 5, 6, 7, 8 Sept. 27, 28, 29, 30
NEW YORK	May 23, 24, 25 July 19, 20, 21, 22 Sept. 5, 6, 7, 8	May 26, 27, 28 July 23, 24, 25, 26 Sept. 9, 10, 11, 12	May 17, 18, 19 July 12, 13, 14, 15 Sept. 17, 18, 19, 20	May 20, 21, 22 July 11 Sept. 13, 14, 15, 16	April 30, May 1, 2 June 30, July 1 Aug. 7, 8, 9 Sept. 29, 30	April 17, 18, 19 June 1, 2, 3 July 28, 29, 30 Sept. 25, 26	*Detroit*	April 20, 21, 22 June 5, 6, 7 July (4), (4) Aug. 10, 11, 12
BOSTON	May 20, 21, 22 July 16, 16, 17, 18 Sept. 13, 14, 15, 16	May 17, 18, 19 July 12, 13, 14, 15 Sept. 17, 18, 19, 20	May 26, 27, 28 July 23, 24, 25, 26 Sept. 9, 10, 11, 12	May 23, 24, 25 July 19, 20, 21, 22 Sept. 5, 6, 7, 8	April 16, 24, 25, 26 June 1, 2, 3 July 28, 29 Sept. (3), (3)	May 29, (30), (30) June 28, 30, July 1 Aug. 7, 8, 9 Sept. 1, 2	April 27, 28, 29 July 2, 3 July 31, Aug. 1, 2 Sept. 22, 23, 24	*News*

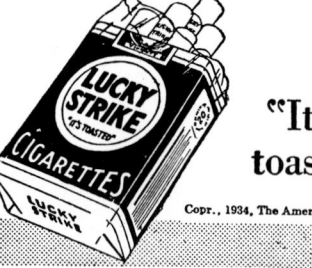

hey fought their way to the Pennant

	1	2	3	4	5	6	7	8	9	10	AB	R	BH	PO	A	E

NAVIN FIELD

Photo by The Detroit News.

Batting, Pitching Records Both Teams

TIGER PITCHERS' AVERAGES

	G	W	L	SO	Pct.
Rowe	44	24	8	150	.750
Marberry	38	15	5	62	.750
Auker	43	15	7	84	.682
Bridges	36	22	11	150	.667
Hogsett	26	3	2	22	.600
Fischer	20	6	4	39	.600
Crowder	38	9	11	68	.450
Sorrell	27	6	9	41	.400
Hamlin	20	2	3	31	.400

TIGERS' INDIVIDUAL AVERAGES

	AB	R	H	Pct.
Gehringer	601	132	214	.356
Greenberg	592	118	201	.339
Cochrane	434	73	141	.325
Owen	563	80	178	.316
White	382	97	120	.314
Rowe	106	14	33	.311
Goslin	617	106	186	.303
Walker	346	54	104	.301
Rogell	594	114	175	.295
Hayworth	167	20	49	.293
Fox	517	100	147	.284
Schuble	15	2	4	.267
Hamlin	25	1	6	.240
Doljack	121	15	28	.231
Hogsett	13	0	3	.231
Marberry	56	7	12	.214
Crowder	62	2	11	.178
York	6	0	1	.167
Auker	73	3	11	.151
Bridges	97	7	12	.124
Clifton	17	3	2	.118
Sorrell	37	1	4	.108
Fischer	31	1	2	.065
Perkins	1	0	0	.000

CARDINAL PITCHERS' AVERAGES

	G	W	L	SO	Pct.
Dizzy Dean	50	30	7	196	.811
Paul Dean	39	19	11	149	.633
Walker	23	12	4	74	.750
Carleton	39	16	11	101	.593
Haines	38	4	4	15	.500
Hallahan	32	8	12	70	.400

CARDINALS' INDIVIDUAL AVERAGES

	AB	R	H	Pct.
Collins	600	115	200	.333
Medwick	620	110	198	.319
Delancey	253	41	80	.316
Frisch	550	73	168	.306
Orsatti	336	40	101	.301
Davis	348	46	104	.299
Martin	450	75	129	.287
Rothrock	643	103	184	.286
Whitehead	332	54	93	.280
Crawford	69	3	19	.275
Durocher	496	61	127	.256
Fullis	297	29	73	.246
J. Dean	118	15	29	.246
P. Dean	83	8	20	.241
Carleton	87	7	17	.195
Hallahan	55	3	10	.182
Haines	19	1	3	.158
Vance	10	2	3	.158
Walker	52	2	5	.096
Mooney	10	0	1	.053

NORTHWESTERN PRINTING CO.